NOBODY WAITING

A German Girl's WWII Story

Annemarie Preussner Korpi

Copyright © 2018 Annemarie Preussner Korpi

All rights reserved.

ISBN: 9781980810568

WHY I LOVE AMERICA

I hungered to come to the greatest country on earth
to embrace the priceless privilege . . . democracy and worth.

I came for your freedom, your justice, your wisdom, your people,
your land I just took it . . . when you reached out your hand.

You inspired my hopes over the years
they were joyful . . . most of my tears.

I toiled I played.
I succeeded, I failed.
I looked at your stars . . .
they never paled.

I laughed and I cried -
to me you are everything . . .
AMERICA you are alright!

You allowed ambitions, dreams and more . . .
All that is worth struggling for.

Thank you for six proud decades with you
Your promises . . . they are all true.

AMERICA, I shall love you forever
I beg you to never deliver me from you . . . never!

-Annemarie Preussner Korpi

CONTENTS

	Acknowledgments	i
1	My Childhood	1
2	The Invasion; Beginning of WWII	19
3	Being a Refugee; It Hurts So Deeply	32
4	Finally; The Americans Free Us From War	89

ACKNOWLEDGMENTS

My thanks to my oldest, deceased son Peter, born in Germany. He gave me the courage to come to America for a better life.

I would like to give special thanks to the many people who helped to make this book possible. I thank my daughters Bernadette and Andrea for always encouraging me to write my story. My special thanks to my son Garret. Without his tireless work this book would not be possible. To my stepdaughter Kimmie a big thank you for graciously putting in a lot of time creating the book cover. Also, my thanks to Rick who prompted the idea of self-publishing. Many thanks to my amazing editor Carol Barkley.

MY CHILDHOOD

"Annemie come sit on my lap. I have something to tell you." Papa tells me that we are going to move soon. He is being transferred from the Czechoslovakian Border to the Polish Border. The name of the village we are moving to is Lindenhorst, in the Province of Silesia. Germany is subdivided into many Provinces, similar to the fifty individual states in the USA.

Both Papa and Mother sound very excited. Papa will be the boss and in charge of Customs operations. The year is 1934 and I am just five years old. Oh, but I would never see Gretel again. We have so much fun and spend so much time together. Every day we walk to the Langsch farm where we both drink one cup full of sweet cream. Our parents say we will never get sick with such healthy nutrition.

Gretel helps me ready all my toys for the movers. When moving day comes both Gretel and I are so sad, and our eyes are all red from crying.

So, this is our new home. The soft beige stucco building contains both our living quarters and the office. Papa introduces us to his new co-workers. There are four desks. Three of the workers live next door with their families. One smaller window in the office faces the gravel road that stretches some two kilometers from the Polish border. Right underneath that window is a good-sized wheel with a handle on it. One worker explains that the wheel operates the barrier over the street. It is always down. It is only put up when a farm wagon with wheat or other crops passes from one country to another. And the loaded goods are always inspected. He points to a long iron rod that is used to poke the loads. This pause is good for the horses also. Sometimes the farmers ask for water for the horses to drink.

"Can I try to crank the wheel?" I ask. "Give it a try," one man says. It is not easy. But I push it hard and the barrier goes up. I think this is really fun.

In one corner of the office is a small chamber, sort of like a small room. "This is the investigation chamber for smugglers," says one man. I don't really understand what that means. Mother takes my hand and says it is time to go. In the entry room stands a big mangle. It also has a big wheel for cranking. "Oh good, now I can run all my linens and other clothes through it when they come off the clothesline. That will be a good job for you, Annemie," says Mother.

The three steps outside also lead to our living quarters. Off the hallway is the living room which connects to the dining room and the other door leads into the kitchen. Its tiled stove and oven combination also has a built-in tub, so there is always warm water for dishwashing and bathing. The two tile ovens in the rooms are very ornate. The color of the tile in the living room is green, and yellow in the dining room. Of course, in the winter those stoves are only used when company is expected or on Sundays for our own use. The only fuel burned is coal. To start the fire, kindling wood has to be carried in from the storage shed where the coals are also stored. It means that it will be my responsibility to carry enough coal and wood into the house to keep it warm and the wood stove going. Boy, I think I am going to be busy.

Adjoining the kitchen is a big wash house with a huge built-in boiler kettle. Mother likes that, for she says she will have the whitest clothes after boiling them in that one. And then beyond

NOBODY WAITING

the tiny entrance is the non-flushing toilet. Good thing it is at the end of the house. I plug my nose. What a stench!

The back door opens to a big grassy yard. A big garden stretches behind the storage shed. The walking path leading through it is lined with flowers such as forget-me-nots, gladiolas, and dahlias and there are also gooseberry and raspberry bushes and currants. "What kind of tree is this, Papa?" "It is a plum tree, Annemie. Isn't it big?" he answers. A wooden fence encloses the entire property.

Mother decides that the two bedrooms upstairs are really all we need. My parents have to pass through my bedroom to get to theirs. "It is good to have two attics. One for storage and the other still has the clothesline up. On rainy days and in the winter time it will help a lot," she says.

"I am so happy we are pretty much settled in. I think I will like it here," Mother comments as she pours Papa's morning coffee. Mother likes things clean and neat. I think she is too fussy! Papa never complains. He is content from day to day. "And my job is coming along fine. The other three Customs officers are nice people," I hear Papa say.

It is fall and my parents think it is a good time for settling in, also a good time for getting to know neighbors and the village with 400 or so people. Then in the springtime, they will plan the planting of the garden.

"Who am I going to play with? There are no kids living nearby." At one farm we buy our milk, eggs, and chickens. They said we may also buy meat and sausages when they butcher a pig. Their daughter Mariele is already six years old. Maybe she could become my friend. She and I will start school in the spring. (In Germany school begins with the first grade.)

Lindenhorst, like all small farm villages, has all their people's houses clustered in one area. All farmers have to drive their horse-drawn wagons to their outlying fields for their work. There is a grocery store, a bakery and a gasthof that we can walk to.

Tomorrow is laundry day. The day before is very busy.

First, we have to do a lot of shopping. Then Mother cooks up a pot of thick soup. She hires a woman from the village to help with the wash. Laundry day lasts all day. Very early in the morning Mother builds a fire under the kettle in the wash house. Everything white goes into the kettle to boil for a long time. Every so often she stirs around in the kettle with a big wooden spoon. The helper lady is working away on the wash board. I never hear them talk. Mother says they need all their breath for the hard work. By afternoon finally, the clothes flap on the clothesline. In the summertime, all the bed sheets are being spread out on the grass and I have to sprinkle water on them from the watering can as soon as they dry. Mother wants them bleached snow white by the sun. In the winter time, all the heavy baskets with the wet laundry have to be carried up to the attic to hang on the clothes line. Sometimes it takes days before they are no longer stiff and are dry. The winter temperature can drop to minus 30 Celsius (minus 22 Fahrenheit). And then when Mother is done sorting and folding all clothes, we take a big basket full to the mangle. It is so hard to turn that wheel and I am so tired at the end of the job.

The following day Mother readies the iron. It is hollow with a door at the end. With a hook, she pulls out a glowing red bolt from the coals in the kitchen stove to slide inside the iron. She has two bolts to interchange to keep the iron hot. So, Mother keeps busy a lot of the time. Some days I get bored. Thankfully laundry day comes only once a month. I am never allowed to go barefoot. The bed must not get dirty. It has to stay clean for four weeks. But when no one sees me I run barefoot across the floor anyway because it feels so good.

***

Sometimes there is a loud knock on the wall from the Office. Mother knows what it means. She has to go next door to inspect a Polish lady who had just come across the border. I overhear my parents when they talk about that. I heard Papa say that sometimes they find big money bills. I think they were often German bills hidden in their knotted hair or in their mouths. The other Customs officials sometimes patrol right along the Polish border. They wear guns across their shoulder. One time they caught a bunch of men and brought them to the Zollamt (Customs office). Mother fixed a lot of coffee and poured it into a big enamel jug. Then she fixed lots of sandwiches for them. They had lard with lots of crackles and salt in between them. When she has to do that I get one of those. The big round eight-pound loaf of rye bread has the largest slice in the middle. I always beg for that one. I can look at it while eating and it lasts a long time. Yummy! Those captured men are smugglers from Poland. Later on, a truck comes and takes them to somewhere. Some things Papa never tells me. So, I don't know where these men are going.

I wake up this morning and it is all white outside. Mother says it is still five weeks until Christmas. Brrr, it is cold outside this morning. The wind blows from the east and brings us the Siberian cold.

It's a good thing the pump is near the back door. When it gets this cold the water freezes. I have to lift the pump cover and pour in warm water. Then I pump like mad till the water starts flowing.

I have to see to the water supply. Three pails sit in the wash house. One is for drinking water, one for cleaning the body and the house. And the empty pail receives the "dump" water which I have to carry outside. Mother and Papa do not want it dumped down into the toilet. They don't want it filled up more than necessary. When the toilet is full the farmer comes with his horses and tank wagon and scoops it empty. He says that is good fertilizer for his fields.

From my upstairs bedroom window, I can see a village with a church high up on the hill. That is across the border in Poland. Today we are expecting visitors from Poland. The Polish Customs official and his family are walking to our house. They have only one daughter and she is even my age. She does not know how to speak German. And I don't know any Polish. Mother tells me that her parents know some German. I am really excited about their visit. Mother says," Now Annemie, you play real nice with Katka." I think about it and look at all my toys. There are really a lot. I never have to share because I have no brothers or sisters. I have them all to myself.

Oh, I will set up my dollhouse, I think to myself. It has a lamp in all three rooms. They even light up. I pack my doll's buggy full with dolls and put the teddy bears on my bed. And I pull the big box with building blocks out from the corner of the room. I can hardly wait for the company to arrive. Then the doorbell rings and we all shake hands. Katka's braids are longer than mine. She has red bows tied into them. She does not say anything, and I don't either. Mother says we can go upstairs and play. We build towers with the blocks. When we demolish them Katka plugs her ears. I laugh. I like playing with her. Katka points to the dollhouse and I nod. After a while, she points to the tea set in the dollhouse. We pretend to have a party. Then Katka tugs on me. She wants me to come to the bed and she smiles at the teddy bears. I don't understand what she is saying. She pulls me along when she is exploring the other bedroom. At my window, she points to her village with a waving gesture. I think she means we can wave at each other's place.

"Annemie and Katka!" Mother calls, "Come down for some cocoa, cake, and whipped cream." When we say goodbye, I gather that next time it is our turn to visit.

***

Christmas is getting closer. Mother has me help her with the baking. I love the good stollen (delicious sweet raisin bread) she makes. I get to cut out the cookies. It is fun to decorate them too. Then Mother hides them from Papa and me because she says there would not be any left for Christmas.

Mother and Papa discuss how many carp we will need for the traditional Christmas Eve dinner. They settle for two. They are being grown in ponds in Poland. A few days before the holidays Papa asks Mother to fill our big zinc bathtub with water. It is put right in the middle of the wash house. Normally it finds its place there every Saturday night for our weekly baths. I go in first and then it is Mother's turn, then Papa. But today the water comes from the pump because the fish like it cold. The carp even smell muddy. Papa says, "We will change the water daily, and by the time Mother cooks them the meat will be so clear and tasty." I spend a lot of time watching them swim. How big they are!

Finally, Christmas day is here. Whatever happens in the living room is behind closed doors. My cheeks are just burning with expectation. By evening Mother has the table set festively. She brings the cooked carp in one piece to the table. It looks to me like it wants to swim away. Mother is a good cook. Potatoes and sauerkraut taste very good with the fish. Papa relishes even the head. He sucks on it and says, "that is the best."

Before the celebration begins in the living room the dishes have to be washed and everything has to be clean.

"Did you hear the bell?" asks Papa. "Santa Claus must have

been here." He opens the living room door. The Christmas tree is full of white candles all aglow. We sing "Stille Nacht". I gaze at the radiant tree. The candles get shorter. Papa says that tomorrow we will have all red candles. Tonight, I may stay up very late. I am so happy about all the many presents. I will never be able to go to sleep.

Many an evening we three go for a walk down the country road. The snow goes crunch, crunch underneath our feet. It is cold. But it looks so light with the full moon. Mother points up to the moon and says, "How clearly we can see the man on the moon." I am awed. I love these winter walks with Papa and Mother. They are always followed with a cup of hot cocoa before bedtime.

***

I am glad it is springtime again. I will be six years old in April. We have befriended two farm families and know them well. Unfortunately, Mariele's parents never let her come to my house. She has so many jobs at home. Mother and I walk to her farm when we are in need of milk. They just have two rooms in their house with all brick floors. The bedroom has three beds. In the kitchen, there are also three beds lined up against the wall. Their grandma lives with them and Mariele has two older brothers. They don't even have electric lights. When they go to the barn they carry kerosene lamps from the house.

Sometimes I come by myself to buy milk, cream or eggs. At least I get to visit a little with Mariele. Her next-door neighbor is real old. "She never comes out of her house," says Mariele. We peek into the window but see nobody. I have never seen a roof like hers. It is made of reef. Mariele says kids try to scare her at night. But the village night watchman is on guard every night and sees to it that nobody harms her. He is an old retired man from the village. Mariele has hardly ever been away from home. Most of her trips are by horse and wagon to the fields to help with work.

The other farm family has no kids. We buy chicken from them, as well as meat and sausage when they butcher a pig.

They mainly raise pigs because they are easy to feed. They get kitchen scraps and they are fed lots of potatoes. I like Frau Hillert. On the way to the grocery store, I often drop in at the Hillerts because I go past their house. When Frau Hillert bakes a big coffee cake she takes some dough and fries it in fat for me. Then she sprinkles sugar on it. That tastes so good. They also have a built-in brick oven to the right of the entryway. When Frau Hillert bakes breads she puts them on a big wooden scoop and shoves them through the opening in the oven. There is room for many of them. It smells so good when she bakes. The other side of the wall has a handle sticking out. Frau Hillert shows it to me and explains that there is a little drum right in the chimney. We fill it with barley seeds and then we crank it till the seeds are roasted. It takes quite a long time. "You can crank it a while if you want to, Annemie." I like the coffee aroma.

One time when I stopped in, the kitchen was full of women. I could hardly see. It looked like a blizzard had gone through the room. They were stripping goose feathers. Feathers and down were just everywhere. Frau Hillert says, "It is just like Grimm's fairy tale. When Frau Holle makes beds in heaven, that's when it snows on earth." I knew that story because Mother or Papa read fairy tales to me at bedtime.

We don't do things like that at our house. I don't really understand why we are not close friends with the people from the village. They are almost all involved in farming. Maybe we are above average in their eyes. When I walk through the village with Papa it sounds like they greet him with a very respectful "Guten Tag, Herr Guderian."

The school is just behind the grocery store. Class starts in April. I will start first grade. I heard that in some countries kids have to go to Kindergarten. This is not how it works in Germany.

A new teacher came to the village. "He is a young bachelor and has a place to live already," says Papa, "but he has no place to eat his meals." "If he likes to he can eat with us," Mother says. And it does work out that way. Herr Langer's transportation is a motorcycle. The agreement is that I can ride with him to school both ways. I am thrilled that I shall ride with my teacher on his motorcycle. He is at school early every morning. He told me I can help him clean blackboards. The night before the first school day I have a hard time falling asleep. My backpack has been carefully assembled. The blackboard has one side with lines and one side with squares. A damp sponge and a dry rag dangle through the hole in the frame. The pencil box has at least two chalk pencils in it.

The next morning the table is set for four people. Herr Langer likes breakfast. I do too. We like a hard, crisp roll with butter and a boiled egg. On the table is liver sausage and tea wurst. That is my favorite. It easily spreads on a hard roll and has a good smoky flavor. Adults drink "real" coffee and I have a cup of barley coffee with cream. At least there is no oatmeal today. I don't like it at all because those grain things get stuck in my throat. When Mother is not looking I try to dump it in the pail. I do like the flour soup that she sometimes makes with milk. She says she makes the lumps on purpose. She does not much stir the flour. And I like that soup. It tastes good with a slice of buttered rye bread.

Papa and Mother wave goodbye as we take off on the motorcycle. My classroom is on the first floor. The higher grades go to the second floor. We get the schedule for April. Every day ends at a different time. Some days are just two hours of lessons and other days are six hours long. Saturday is mostly just two hours. When I am out early I walk home. I like school and I like most kids. When I get home on the first day Papa is outside with the camera in his hands. Mother gives me two huge, pretty paper bags filled with candy and goodies. "That is a reward for being a school girl now," she says with a smile.

One evening after supper Papa shows Mother a drawing for the garden planting. Next time we go to the grocery store we buy lots of seeds. "In May, we will get some plants to put in the ground," I hear Mother say. "This garden will keep us busy all summer long. I will have a lot of canning to do in the fall,

Annemie. But the fruit sauces will make a good desert in the winter time. The raspberry jam will taste good for breakfast."

One afternoon as I am outside with Mother some boys from school walk by. They are in second grade already. "Annemie, do you want to play with us?" they call. "Mother, please, may I?" She answers, "You have almost one hour till suppertime." Playing with boys is much more exciting. Narrow as the wooden fence is across, we manage to walk on it. One boy falls off more often than I do. But I am not the one who climbs in the highest branches of the plum tree. Just when we are in the middle of hide and seek Mother calls, "Annemie, time to eat." The boys have to go home now.

Sunday is here again. The nearest Catholic Church is in the next village, a three-kilometer walk on a country gravel road. The best thing about it is the sandwiches Mother brings for the walk home. When we arrive at church sometimes it is so crowded that we cannot find a seat. I am tired standing up throughout mass after our walk. This village, Goschitz, has a big Estate surrounded by concrete walls. It is the home of a Baron who owns vast acres of land. A lot of poor people work for him. They live in community housing. When the Baron arrives late for mass the priest waits for him. This only extends our time to wait. When he walks in, all the people rise as though he were God. I feel it is so unfair to have to wait for him till I almost faint. Why does the Baron think he is so important? There is no way Papa thinks himself better than the peasants.

***

By now it is summer vacation. We have four weeks. And then in the fall and for Easter we get another three weeks off. It is a hot summer day, but Papa is determined to build an arbor next to the back door. It is made of young birch trees, sort of open and he is going to grow grapevines all over it. "Annemie, it will give us some shade and be big enough for a picnic table. Mother can clean the vegetables from the garden right here. And you, Annemie, can sit out here on nice days and do your homework," he says. We do not have mosquitoes. They stay in the woods. We are quite used to the flies. The curtains across the open windows keep them out of the house.

***

We have lived here almost three years. Some of the fall days are still warm enough to sit outside in the arbor. Now that I am in third grade I have to do my homework on paper with a pencil. Papa is so strict when it comes to doing homework. He always tears up my paper if I did not do it perfectly. My first-grade teacher Herr Langer is married by now and well cared for. Since Papa plays the violin he has a second one for me to learn on. I am practicing every day. Pretty soon we play a duet and I like the sound of it. By Christmas time we will play seasonal music together. That will be fun.

***

"I cannot believe it is spring already," Mother declares. She kisses me goodbye before I leave for school. When I return home, a car is parked in front of the Zollamt (Customs office). I ask Mother whose it is. She says, "It is ours: yours and Papa's and mine." What a surprise! My first thought is that we don't have to walk to church anymore. Papa knows how to drive a car. He takes Mother out every day until she is ready to get her driver's license.

Sometimes we take a trip to the big city of Breslau. It is the capital of our province of Silesia. Half a million people live there. The car is a DKW (Deutscher Kraftwagen). It looks like it is made of pressed cardboard. The color is a purplish brown.

On our first trip to Breslau, I get to bring my pillow and a blanket. The whole back seat is mine. It is some 60 kilometers to Breslau and it takes us almost two hours. I have never been in such a big city. Some buildings are so tall. Huge apartment buildings are five stories high. The streets are full of cars and people.

Papa drives the car into a parking lot. When we stop at a restaurant, my parents drink something and order a very small egg liqueur for me. I like it. It is thick and sweet. At home Mother gives me a raw whipped egg every day. She adds sugar and lemon or a little bit of dark beer to it.

After lunch, we go shopping. I hold on tight to Mother's hand. I don't want to get lost here. That would be really scary. The stores are so big. We go up to a higher floor on a moving stair, called an escalator. I beg for more rides and am allowed to do it. I look so much at everything that I wish I had more eyes. The day goes by much too fast. By early evening we are on our way home. I am so tired when I settle into my backseat. Clouds and trees and many lights go by just for a little while and when I wake up, we are at home.

When I am at school Mother drives to Festenberg, the nearest small town with just some eight thousand people, eight kilometers away. Every time she drives there she asks me what I would like her to bring back. My answer is the same always; "A creampuff like you brought the first time you went." I really feel we are the wealthiest family in the village. I don't know of anyone who owns a car. The neighbors are happy, too, because they ride along to church on Sundays.

The following week Hans, Paul, and Herbert challenge me on the way home from school. "You can't jump across the wide part of the ditch like we can!" Well, I am going to prove to them that I can, too. But it does not take long, and I slide backward in the mud with my good dress. And it is so important to Mother that I always look neat and clean. Now I am all mud coated. My new shoes don't even show their blue color anymore. But jumping is sort of fun and I have to do it till I can make it all the way across. It takes lots of practice. The boys cheer me on.

"Where have you been all this time? Mother and I worried about you!" Papa says. He takes another look at me and just marches me home. My heart is pumping fast all the way. I know what is going to happen. There will be no escape from that carpet beater. I never tried ditch jumping again, not with pretty, new clothes on.

Because of my naughtiness, I want to be in compliance and don't even complain when I have to go to the basement to get potatoes or carrots. I hate having to do that. After the fall harvest, these vegetables are stored in a large pile of sand down there to keep them from freezing. The mice also live in the basement. Every time I have to go down I sing at the top of my lungs, so it echoes, and I cannot hear the scurrying mice. My whole body goes into goosebumps.

To collect tea is a much nicer job. Late in the summer, it is easy to find chamomile plants. My nose tells me where the peppermint plants grow. The Yarrow plant is higher and easier to see. Mother has a way of drying those plants. In the wintertime, they make a warming drink. And Mother says they also remedy sicknesses. I much prefer a hot cup of cocoa with cream floating on top, especially after sleigh riding.

In late winter I become so sick with the flu. I think Mother's cure most merciless. First, she makes me drink lots of hot tea. It is Linden blossom tea, sweetened with honey. Then she rolls me totally into a big blanket. On top of that, she covers me with the big featherbed. She says, "Now you can really sweat it all out and you will be well in no time, Annemie." I have never been as miserable as I am now. I am not even able to move. Bad thoughts enter my mind. How can Mother be so mean? I am totally helpless. I have to abide by Mother's no-nonsense prescription. Of course, I have never figured out why it did not kill me. I recovered instead. Before you see a doctor, you have to be half dead. There is an effective herb for every illness. Or so everybody believes.

When I have to go to the grocery store I sometimes pull my sled. Right behind the store, there is a short hill. There are mostly other kids sliding too. It is so much fun. But I don't know to stop when I get cold. I think it is easier for boys to keep warm. They are wearing pants. Girls just wear homemade stockings. Mother knits all of mine. But the knees get wet in no time. So sometimes by the time I get home I am almost crying because my knees hurt so badly. Mother makes me take off the stockings and my knees are red and bumpy. A tub big enough for me to kneel in is filled with warm water. It sure eases the pain. It is all forgotten next time I go sliding again. But I do try to be more careful.

***

It is New Year's Day, 1939 already. Today we are invited again to Katka's house in Poland. It is just two kilometers to the border and then another kilometer to her house. Her father is also involved in Customs in Poland. During all our visits I have learned a few Polish phrases as she has German ones. So, we communicate a lot better. We have a good meal at their house. Polish dumplings with pork roast and cabbage. Then we bundle up, for Katka takes me for a walk through her village. Katka is Catholic also. In Silesia, the population is 60% Lutheran and the others are Catholic. I don't know of any other religions. Katka says that most Poles are Catholic. We even stop in at the church. It is so pretty. It has more of the Virgin Mary and saint statues than our church. It does not take us long to walk through the whole village. We can think of a lot to do but there is never enough time. So, we have to say goodbye once more.

One day when I come home from school Mother says, "Papa wants to see you right away." Pretty soon he steps out of the office. He looks angry, all red in the face and asks, "Annemie, who were you with when you threw mud all over Hitler's picture?" A big Hitler picture hangs under the overhang in the middle of the outside wall of the building. I answer, "With nobody. I didn't even know that there is mud all over the picture." Papa does not believe me. I have never seen him so mad. He takes me in the house. With the carpet beater in his hand, he grabs me by my underwear and hits me on the butt till the underwear is in threads. He even yells at Mother. "I could lose my job over this and be hauled off by the Nazis." I don't fully understand why he is so furious. My pride is hurt even more than my butt. I really did not do it. It is a bad day and my sobs go on for a long time. I am sent to bed early and without supper. We never talk about it again.

***

These last March days of 1939 bring back the birds, the grass, and the buds. Wearing just a spring jacket almost makes me skip down the road. I have to get two dozen eggs from the Heider Farm. Mariele is outside. I say, "Guten Tag, Mariele, what are you doing?" She has knives and forks and spoons in a pail of water. She dips a wet rag into fine sand and rubs it along the silverware. "See how shiny they get?" she says with a proud joy. "I have to do this twice a month. Otherwise, they get real rusty and the food does not taste good. My mother cleans them in the wintertime in the house."

"Are you going to middle school in Festenberg after Easter vacation, Annemie?" "Yes, I am," I say. "My parents made that decision. I guess if you don't start middle or high school as of fifth grade you have to remain in elementary school and you are finished after grade eight. Then what would you do? You are too young to get married, ah? And going to trade school really is more for boys. I wish you could go too, Mariele." She almost sulks because she would love to go, too. She says her parents cannot afford it. It costs 20 German marks for every month. "I will have to ride my bicycle. I am really a little scared. It will take me at least one hour every morning and the same time riding home. And I am all by myself."

Slowly I become accustomed to the daily bike rides to school. It is a hard work out to pump on the gravel road till Goschitz, which is halfway to school. The latter half is an asphalt road. That part of the ride I don't mind at all. On rainy days Papa or Mother gives me a ride. I also have a rain cape with a hood. It covers even the handlebar and protects my school bag with the books. It is a lonely ride, though. Occasionally a horse-drawn wagon passes me or comes from the opposite direction. One time, outside of Goschitz a wagon loaded high with hay had its horses galloping out of control straight toward me. No driver could be seen. I screamed. I got off the bike so fast and crossed the ditch and ran into the open field. Way in the distance I saw the wagon slow down and then stop. That was a scare.

The bicycle is Mother's old one. Too often I have a flat tire. I carry a pump. After I pump air into the tire it will ride a while again. But I am not always that lucky. That means I have to push it home. Good thing it always happens on the way home. There is a blacksmith just where I enter our village. He fixes my bike right away while I wait. When he is in the middle of shoeing a horse, I have to wait. I don't mind because I like to watch the sparks fly when he shapes the shoes.

It is a summer Sunday and Mother and Papa collect our handled baskets and go for our walk in the woods which stretch mainly along the border. The pine trees smell so good. It feels like you can take much deeper breaths than you normally can. I like that past time. We gather mushrooms and always seem to have a contest to see whose basket fills up first. My favorites are "Pfifferlinge". They are yellow and solid. Because of their color, they are easy to find. "Steinpilze" I also like. They are bigger and have a brown cap. Mother warns me not to even touch the pretty looking redheads with the white dots. "They are very poisonous," she says. On the walk home, we hum "Ein

Maennlein steht im Walde" (a little man stands in the forest). Every child knows that song. It depicts the beauty of that poisonous mushroom.

Then for supper Mother fries lots of onions in butter and adds the sliced mushrooms. It tastes yummy on a big slice of rye bread.

THE INVASION

BEGINNING OF WWII

The last August days are cooling off. The farmers are busy in their fields. Papa and Mother spend a lot of time in the garden. Often, they stop talking when I come around. Papa says, "You can go and play a while, Annemie. Mother and I have to talk about something." Boy, I think, something is different. I just cannot figure out what it is.

Sunday before bedtime Papa and Mama want me to sit with them. They say they have to tell me something very important. "You will not go to school tomorrow. Tomorrow our backyard will be filled with soldiers. Even a cannon will be there. The next day might be very active and exciting." "Why will there be a cannon? Will they shoot?" I ask. "We hope not," says Papa. "It is just a precaution in case the enemy attacks." I ask, "What does that mean, Papa?" "There will be a war, just a short war. Germany is invading Poland." "Why, Papa?" I ask. "Our Fuehrer, Adolph Hitler," he says reflectively, "decided that. I cannot really tell you why, because I do not know."

It is very hard to go to sleep. I am full of anticipation. What it will be like tomorrow, I wonder? I can't really comprehend it all.

When I wake up in the morning I stretch and roll over.

Mother has not come to wake me yet. I remember that I don't have to go to school today. I get out of bed and as I look out of the window I see soldiers moving around in the yard. I think of last night's talk with Papa and Mother. They were right. I pull the curtain aside and there is something standing in the middle of the yard. It is all covered up with lots of green branches. That must be the cannon they were talking about.

I run down the stairs into the kitchen. "Mother, you were right last night. I did not think that this would really happen. Can I go outside and talk to the soldiers?" I ask. "First you eat some breakfast. Then I will take you outside and introduce you. I do not want you to be from home at all today. Who knows, we may even have to go into the cellar," she says. "Why do we have to go into the cellar?" I ask. "Just in case of some unrest. Nobody knows, though, that there is a cannon in the yard. That's why it is so camouflaged." I ask what that means. Mother explains that all the green branches on the cannon make it look like a tree and nobody can tell that there is a cannon underneath the branches.

After I force some oatmeal down, Mother takes me outside and tells the soldiers that I am her daughter Annemie and that I am 10 years old.

"Guten Morgen (good morning), Annemie," they say and they are very friendly. "You can watch us if you like." I am very uneasy, but this is too exciting to miss. Mother allows me to stay out here, as long as I don't leave the yard. "I trust you will keep an eye on Annemie," I hear her saying.

One man says, "We will set up a canteen soon and you can join us if you like and you can even line up for dinner with us, Annemie. Do you like split pea soup?" I nod my head. "I like it," I answer. "Alright, Annemie, would you pump some water for us? We will need a lot of it." While I pump water, I am still trying to figure out what is going on. Are our friends in Poland still our friends? Will we see them again?

This canteen is odd looking. It has four legs with a big kettle on top. It is set up near the pump. One soldier is busy with it all the time. He puts lots of food in it and pours in the water I bring to him. The other soldiers say that he is the most important man. If he does not do a good job cooking food for them, they will fire him. And they all laugh. I am not sure if I want to stay outside with them or go into the house. They are sprawled out all over our backyard. The sky is clear, and the thermometer shows 17 degrees Celsius. They say that next to the arbor is their bedroom. There is a pile of sleeping bags. Part of the woodshed stores their guns. They keep the doors closed and tell me to stay out of it. They do not want me to get hurt.

Two army jeeps and a truck are parked alongside the house. "Why are you all here? How long are you going to stay?" I ask. They just say, "Higher Commands."

They don't know. They are jolly, and they laugh a lot. I count them and there are eleven men in the yard. They are from different areas in Germany.

Mother calls me in for dinner, but the soldiers say, "Annemie is going to eat with us. But you can go and get a dish and spoon for yourself. Bring something unbreakable," they add. They all have aluminum dishes. The dish has two attached handles with a top and bottom. They say the food does not spill when they carry it because they can cover the dish. The cups are aluminum too. As we stand in line I hear one soldier say, "I wish she were older." I do not know what to think of that. Why does he want me to be older?

The canteen is full with good split pea soup. It tastes very good with lots of bacon in it. A thick slice of buttered rye bread would have gone good with it.

They ask me a lot of questions about the Polish village. "Do I know it? Do I know many people from there?" I tell them about my friend.

Soon they line up by the pump and wash all their dishes clean. "That was a late dinner," they say. It is already half past three in the afternoon. "But there are no regular hours when you are in the army." Our toilet sure gets used a lot. I don't know if my parents like that. At day's end, I am just as confused as I was in the morning. Nothing is clear to me.

In the past days or even weeks, quite a few cars were parked in front of the Zollamt. Sometimes they even came in big chauffeur-driven cars from Breslau. One time, two of those men even ate in our dining room with Papa. Mother spent no more time in there than it took to serve the meal. The dining room door was always closed.

Toward evening Mother prepares the living room couch into a bed. "Who is going to sleep here?" I ask. "We have to accommodate two officers," Mother says. "We have to in our house?" I ask. "Yes, we have been ordered to do so." I sure don't understand it all.

The next morning Mother wakes me. "Time to get up, Annemie. Breakfast is ready. Any time now our troops will come marching by here and continue toward Poland." Today is Friday, September 1, 1939. Mother calls it the Invasion Day. "Where is Papa?" I want to know. "He is very busy. He went to the office very early when it was still dark outside," is the answer. The soldiers in the backyard seem very busy, too. Mother won't even let me go outside.

We go upstairs to make our beds. I don't want to stay downstairs alone. The officers went to the Zollamt early, too. Mother cleans up the couch in the living room. This is just not a normal day (again).

"Let's look out the front door, Annemie." There are one, two cars parked in front of the Zollamt. Officers scramble back and forth.

It is not much later when soldiers come marching from the direction of the school. There is an endless line of them. They all carry rifles across their shoulders. It is a scary sight! Some limp but they keep moving. They see us. They ask how much further it is to the Polish Border. "Two kilometers," says Mother. They stir up a lot of dust on the gravel road.

"We have walked many hours already. Would you have some water for our canteens?" they ask. Mother and I get a water pail each and pump it full with water. We put a ladle into each and carry it out to the street. We try to fill as many canteens for the men as we can. They momentarily slow down but they keep moving all the time. I go back and forth to fill a pail while Mother does the ladling.

All the soldiers look so exhausted. Their helmets look heavy. Sometimes a man lifts it off to wipe his head with a brown handkerchief. I am losing track of time. But it takes a very long time before the line of men ends. Slowly we can see them disappearing in the direction of Poland.

Papa walks out of the office with some officers. Before he gets into the car with them he tells Mother not to worry. He will be back soon, and he waves at me. Mother looks very worried. She takes me very tightly by the hand. I want to hold on to her all the time. I am scared.

In school, we have been taught that we must always look up to our Fuehrer Adolph Hitler. He is a great leader. Every morning we have to salute with "Heil Hitler" with our right arm raised. So, why do I have to look up to him? All these men marching by today did not look so happy. I would much rather be in school. Something about all that is happening just does not feel right.

With the empty pails Mother and I return to the house. Tears are rolling down Mother's cheeks. She says, "This is the beginning of a war." I want to know what is going to happen. But she has no answer for me. "Maybe Papa can tell us when he gets back," she says absent-mindedly. She wants me to go upstairs with her. Perhaps she thinks we can figure out things better from the upper windows. It is quiet in the yard. All the soldiers but four are gone. The cannon still sits there. The men look like they are ready to shoot it any moment. They just don't seem as carefree as they were yesterday. From my bedroom window, we look toward Poland. The church stands on top of a hill. Its steeple reaches high into the sky. Mother is worried about Papa. "I hope that he is coming back as soon as they said they would." I feel uneasy, too.

"Will you come with me to the bathroom, Mother? I am

scared to be alone." So, we go downstairs. It feels almost eerie to walk through the house. I still can't make any sense of it all. If only Papa were here, I would not be so scared.

We look at the clock. It is almost 12 o'clock noon. Mother wants to go upstairs again to look toward Poland. As we look out the window we can make out the German flag flying from the church steeple. "Oh, my God," Mother exclaims with her hands thrust above her head. "The swastika is flying from the Catholic church in Poland. That will not bring any blessing to our country or our people!"

Papa does come back a bit later. Mother is so happy that she cries. I hear Papa say, "Thank God there was no resistance, none. It all happened so fast and unexpectedly. They did not have time to think over there. They were told if they remain peaceful no harm will come to them." After he stood a while quietly, he gravely said, "I don't like this, I don't like what is happening. We will have to do some planning. I want you and Annemie away from here. Let's all hop into the car and drive to Festenberg. I want to mail a telegram to the grandparents in Berlin. First, we will buy two train tickets, so we can inform them of your arrival. The Customs operations are not going to be as they were. But I am on alert all the time. I don't know exactly what is going to happen next."

The night is peaceful. The next day Mother and I are on the train. But I can't empty my head yet of all the things that took place the past few days.

Papa's sister Gertrude, her husband and my two cousins Hans and Eva live in the same house with Papa's parents. Opa (grandpa) and Oma (grandma) are awaiting us. Their beautiful house is in the Berlin suburb of Hermsdorf, the yard surrounded by a concrete wall. From the second story window, the view faces a lake in the middle of a park. Eva says, "We will go there often for walks." Eva is also 10 years old and Hans is only eight years old. We all walk to the same school together. It takes us just ten minutes. It is not that hard to adjust to the kids and the teacher. I am right in with Eva's friends. Of course, I have to tell in front of the class how I was on the Polish border on September 1st when our troops marched by our house on the way to Poland.

***

Mother is going back. She knows that I am in good hands. She will write and expects me to write often.

In her last letter, Mother lets me know that she has found an apartment in Breslau. The Zollamt is no longer in operation. The troops are in charge of border operations. Papa has to serve in Poland now. She writes that he is annexed to the German army. It is the beginning of November. Mother will come for Christmas. Then we will leave together right after the holidays.

Papa will also spend Christmas with us if he can. After we arrive in Breslau, which is the capital city of the province of Silesia, I can start school there. My first thoughts are that I will not know anyone in school again. I begin to dread that. But I will like to be home with Mother again.

***

New Year's Day, 1940. The apartment is nice. Off the big hallway is a good-sized living room with a balcony facing the main street. It is in the eastern suburb of Breslau, called Scheitnig. We are on the third floor. "We will not lack any exercise, carrying wood and coal up from the basement for heating. Every apartment has a small storage room assigned," Mother explains.

From our balcony, we could see the streetcars go by. Back in Berlin I sometimes rode the subway. They always came on time. We did not fool around while boarding. The doors promptly closed after the last person was inside. I could never figure out how they knew when to close the door.

It is cold in the small kitchen. Maybe it is just the tile floor. But it is so modern. We cook with gas. And there is one bedroom. In the bathroom, the tank above the bathtub also has to be heated with wood and coals before taking a bath. Mother says, "We will have to take baths sparingly because of fuel shortage. Every household is being rationed. Most of the supplies are being saved for the army."

I have to take the streetcar to school. It is too far to walk. Mother comes with me the first day. I am accepted at the Lyceum (high school for girls only). My schedule is busier than it was before. I again have the English class. I can choose to partake in French and Spanish at the start of sixth grade. That will begin in April. I think I will opt for French. I really enjoy learning the English language. It is my most favored class.

Some of my classmates I really like. Gisela is in with one group of friends and they let me join them. Gisela lives a few kilometers from my house. We become good friends. When we visit each other, we have to ride the streetcar. After spring vacation, we elect the same classes and share a lot of time together. Gisela has only one sister. She is much older and has a job already. So, Gisela is almost alone like I am.

When I come home today Mother is joyful. She shows me a letter from Papa. It comes from Krakau, Poland, where Papa is stationed. It is at least 300 kilometers away. "Papa is furloughed for almost a week," she says. He is coming by train. Our car has been confiscated by the German army shortly after the invasion and we have never seen it since.

When Papa arrives, it is a happy day. He has a bunch of gifts for us; for me a wonderful pair of shoes. The color is navy. They fit, and I just love them. They are wide enough for my wide feet. He also has yards of fabric. He knows that Mother is a good seamstress. That means that she might sew a pretty dress for me. For Mother, he has a blouse and a beautiful scarf and gloves. It is so nice to have him home. I wish he could just stay. I ask him what he is doing in Krakau. However, he does not talk about his job. I think he just does not want me to know so I don't worry. I ask if he knows anything about Katka and her parents. He says, "No, they left their home pretty soon after the invasion." He does not know where they are.

His leave goes by much too fast. He says he will write often and come again when he can.

But in time his letters become less frequent. With the passing years, nothing becomes more plentiful. Food rationing becomes scarcer all the time.

Gisela and I attend the weekly Hitler Jugend (youth) meetings. They are boring. We just sit around and talk about Hitler and all his victories. We must sacrifice, we are told.
We will win the war. I plead with Mother to not have to be part of those meetings anymore. She finally gives in. Soon a personal letter is addressed to her saying, "If your daughter, Annemie, misses more meetings she may be visited at a concentration camp next time." It is sent by the Nazi Party. Mother is shaking while reading this.

Gisela has been more loyal to the Hitler Jugend than I have been. "From now on you will go to every meeting," says Mother. We have to wear uniforms. The skirt is navy blue, the blouse white with a black tie-like scarf pulled through a brown leather knot. Sometimes when an important dead hero's casket is brought through Breslau for the burial, we, the Hitler Jugend, have to line the street and salute with the "Heil Hitler" greeting. We have to keep the right arm straight up till it hurts.

☐

Annemie's Hitler Youth Photo

Jews are being mistreated. They are not allowed inside the streetcar. They may only ride on the outside of the car. They also are not allowed to walk on the sidewalk, only on the street. They all are identified by the yellow Jewish star they have to wear at all times. It is made of fabric. They have to wear it on their outer clothing for identification. At our Hitler Jugend meeting, we were told one time that it is all right to spit on Jews when walking past them. They are not worthy people. They are not deserving of our great Fuehrer. When Mother heard me relate that to her she became quite disturbed about it. "Never do I want you to do anything like that," she said. "They are good people just like we are. I remember my best and most capable doctor from the small town I grew up in," she added. "He was Jewish."

I'm already in ninth grade. The war has begun almost four years ago. The German troops are deep in Russia. They are also fighting in Italy and advancing into Africa. Great Britain is being bombarded all the time. They are also fighting on the western front in France and the Netherlands. On the radio, we hear that Germany is winning on all fronts. "How is this all going to end?" Mother mumbles. She says, "Annemie, you and I are going to share a secret. You promise me that you will never tell this to anyone, not even to Gisela?" I say, "Yes, Mother, I do." She makes sure the living room door is closed and the apartment door is locked. She is then searching for Radio Free Europe. They broadcast in German. We have our ears glued to the radio. We want to make sure nobody can hear. What a different story we learn. The German army suffers defeats on all fronts, they say.

We get a letter from Papa today. It is backdated three months. It's just about one-half a year ago since we heard last. Papa does not report much in his writing. It does not sound like him. It appears that letters have been lost in between writings. We cannot really figure out what is happening to him.

The next letter requests Mother to avail herself for work for the Vaterland (Fatherland). She is to report to the hospital. It is right across the busy street from us. Practically every change one makes in Germany has to be reported to an authority, so a person's workplace or residence is always known. I heard it said once that the country stays "pure" that way. That is how they knew how to get hold of Mother.

So, the next morning while I get ready for school, Mother readies herself to report at the hospital. At day's end, she tells me that she will have to work six-days-a-week. Help is hard to get. Mother's job will be to register admissions. She has good handwriting and the admission desk is extremely busy with all the wounded soldiers arriving. Mother does not mind at all. She says that we can use the additional cash. Papa's salary is automatically transferred to the local bank. "On the other hand," Mother adds, "we can hardly buy anything with the money." The stores are getting empty. Everything has to go to the frontlines. Our food supply is getting less and less.

Gisela comes to my house right after school because I am home alone. We like being by ourselves. Sometimes we want to eat something. There is only dry bread. One time we make ourselves a roux because we find enough flour and margarine. It tastes delicious.

Next time Gisela comes we walk across the street to visit Mother. We see lots of uniforms. All the patients we see are soldiers. They come from the Eastern Front. Breslau, on the Oder River, is the largest city centrally located in the easternmost part of Germany. Mother says she is very busy registering all the admissions. She asks one soldier with kitchen duties if there is any food left over. "Sure," he says and walks Gisela and me to the kitchen. There is a big pot with a hot dish. He fills two plates for us. He even gives us a slice of bread. Does it ever taste good! He says, "Come again." "Thank you, we sure will," is our answer. We both think he is not only nice, he is also good looking.

Next week in school I have bad luck. In Home Economics class we learn how to crochet. We have fine cotton yarn and a thin crocheting needle. We line up to show the teacher our accomplishment. We push and fool around a lot. All of a sudden, the hook I am holding is jabbed into my left wrist by at least one centimeter. Ouch, that does not feel good. The worst thing is that I cannot pull it out. So, the teacher wants me to walk to a nearby hospital. "Who wants to go with Annemie?" she asks. Gisela volunteers immediately. Of course, there is no transportation. So, I have to walk. I can't even get my arm through my coat sleeve with that hook sticking out. At the hospital in the hallway is a long line of people. I have to sit in line and wait and wait. Loads of stretchers with wounded soldiers are wheeled past us. We are told as soon as they are cared for it will be our turn. My wrist is swelling. My biggest worry is that I don't know how to notify Mother. In the late afternoon, the doctor numbs my wrist and pulls the hook out. He bandages the wrist and puts it into a sling.

When I get off the streetcar at home it is dusk already. Mother is almost out of her mind with worry. "Where in the world have you been?" She is crying. She is so relieved that I am back. I tell her about all the things that have happened to me.

Our next-door neighbor, Frau Wendel, is a nice lady. Her husband is also in the service. They have two little girls. Frau Wendel is telling Mother she is expecting a baby and she is going to live temporarily in the country with some relatives. She leaves her key with Mother. "We will miss you, Frau Wendel. I wish you well, though. Hopefully, the war will be over soon, and we will see you again."

***

Christmas 1944! Just Mother and me. We don't even hear from Papa anymore. All is bad and sad.

I can't believe I am in 10th grade. Nor can I say that I have learned much this past year. Everything revolves around the war. "Don't go home and tell your parents that you are hungry," one Nazi teacher kept saying. "The food is needed for our soldiers to fight and win the war." And then we did drills to prepare us for wearing a gas mask. It amused us because we thought we all looked like we were wearing a pig's head.

Schools no longer have fuel. Christmas vacation is extended into the sixth week. Mother does not go to the hospital anymore. She says it is getting chaotic over there, from bookkeeping to patient care. The winter is bitterly cold. When the wind blows from the east it sends shivers down my spine.

☐

BEING A REFUGE

IT HURTS SO DEEPLY

This January of 1945 is extremely cold. It feels so cozy under the featherbed. The apartment is cold. Little fuel is left. Little food is left. Rations have become so tiny. Mother keeps saying that it is not enough for a dying person. How are we supposed to keep alive?

I sleep in my Dad's bed. Two single beds share the head and foot boards. That's comfortable sleeping.

These past two years were meager ones. I am not even out of bed yet and my stomach makes loud, growling noises. The stores may as well have been closed since weeks before the Christmas of 1944. Nothing is available anymore. No clothes, no food, no fuel. Dad's letters have stopped coming altogether.

"Annemie, your oatmeal is ready." "I am coming, Mother." Brrr ... it is cold. I am opening the still-pulled shades. The patio door faces east. No sun today. But what is going on out there? "Mother, come here! Come and see what is happening!" "Was ist denn los? (What is the matter?)" she asks.

"Look at that ... Look at that trek out there! It is endless!" I have never seen anything like this. Big wagons, horses, even oxen hitched to them. They are pulling heavy loads. People are walking behind. It is hard to see their faces. They are so bundled up. It is very cold. Children on the wagons are surrounded by featherbeds. Belongings are piled high on the wagons.

Tears are running down Mother's face. "All these people are running away from home," she says. So, the faint sounds of thundering we have been hearing were sounds of war. I feel forlorn. I sense fright. My stomach feels knotted up. We just stand there helplessly. We watch. There is no break in the thread of wagons. They move slowly. Both people and animals look so exhausted.

"Where are they going, Mother?" Barely audible, she says, "They move west, away from the enemy, away from the Russians, just away from the enemy." "Can't we help, Mother?" I ask. "How can we help?" she replies.

The oatmeal is long cold by now. We do not feel like eating anyhow. We get dressed. Outside our apartment door the hall is silent. The neighbors left a long time ago. The apartment below us is occupied by an elderly couple. They are dumbfounded by our testimony of the outside. They show little reaction. We will see what the other neighbors think. But no one answers the door. Where is everybody? Have they left town? We really don't know anybody well. The place is deserted.

We slowly climb back up the steps. We feel a bit uneasy in our apartment.

How can I contact my friends or even just one of them? None of them live nearby. Nobody has a telephone. I don't think that streetcars run per schedule with all the confusion in the streets. How can anything function? "I don't know what to do, Annemie," says Mother. "Let me walk to Gisela's house, Mother. Maybe her family knows what to do." "No," Mother almost yells. "I will not let you leave this house."

We turn on the radio. It is playing music as always. "Let's scan for Radio Free Europe, Mother. Remember how we heard months ago that the German troops were slowly driven back in Russia? And our station reported at the same time how victorious the German troops were?"

As we did in the past, we put our heads close to the radio.

We are still afraid that somebody could hear us. It has happened that people were sent to concentration camps for listening to Radio Free Europe. We scan the scale over and over. But no luck. We just hear the same old propaganda. The German troops are conquering the enemy everywhere. We are told that again and again.

The picture outside has not changed. The wagon wheels are slowly turning. The people almost fall over their tired feet.

"You know what I am going to do, Annemie?" "No, what?"

"I will boil some water and make tea. Find something big to pour it into." I suggest, "How about the can we buy milk in? It has a cover and the enamel won't break". "That's good," says Mother. We put on our winter wear and leave with the still hot tea.

As we approach the moving line we hear little children's cries. There doesn't seem to be any younger men; there are just women, old men, young and older children. This sad site is overwhelming. Mother holds up the can. "Here is some hot tea." A boy, maybe ten years or so, holds out a dented aluminum cup. Mother fills it up. They move so slowly, we just walk alongside.

"Where are you from?"

Without any expression, the woman says, "We come from Oels." She continues walking behind the wagon. Oels is halfway between Breslau and the Polish border.

They must all be farmers. They all have featherbeds on top of their loads. Kids in between them just stare or whine. Dishes stick out from underneath the blankets. More cups are being extended toward us. The tea disappears fast.

"Where are you going?" Mother asks another woman.

"We had to leave. The Russian front was coming close to home. The shooting sounds were coming closer and closer." These German people are fleeing from the Russians, the enemy. "And where are you going now?" Mother asks again. "I don't know," the woman utters, pointing ahead.

The trot of the horses continues. We are left with our

thoughts. Half a block away is home. These peoples' home is a moving wagon with no certain destination. Thank God this is not happening to us. Oels is only some 30 kilometers east of here. No, the enemy front just cannot penetrate our homeland any deeper. I don't want to think about it. Hitler got us into this mess.

Mother is silent. The pale white snow cover suddenly turns ghastly and fits our sullen mood. A few other onlookers on the sidewalk were looking sad ... tragic ... miserable.

It is Sunday. Well, maybe things will be normal again. We are ready for a cup of tea and a sandwich. There is a small chunk of Harzer Roller, a semi-soft stinky cheese, left. Ja, our party leaders tell us all the time that we must sacrifice food for our fighting soldiers. Our growling stomachs don't conform to that kind of thinking, though.

We busy ourselves. Mother does some hand sewing. One skirt needs hemming and a button came off my coat. She had an old drab gray wool blanket that she died navy. She transformed it into a stylish mid-length coat for me.

I pull out the darning basket. It is always full of stockings. I don't own a pair of stockings without runs or holes. The rayon has no resilience to wear. I wish I owned one pair without big patches! Oh, someday the war will end. Then it will be fun to go shopping, I think.

Usually, Mother and I hum and harmonize our favored songs to such activity, but not today. There is a hushed-up feeling. We don't intrude upon each other's thoughts.

"I will heat water and fill the hot-water bottles. Mother, are you cold, too?" "Go ahead," she says, "and make a cup of hot tea."

I wonder how the people we saw outside are doing. It is afternoon and there is just one wagon going by now and then. Somehow, I tell myself that the misery will be ending for all the people out there. Soon they can go home, and the war will be over.

It is almost four o'clock. It is still cloudy. The day is dark and gloomy. We sip our tea, waiting for it to get dark enough to turn on the lights. Of course, we are expected to use the least possible electricity. The street lights are never lit. The whole city is in total darkness all night. No window must ever show light. This is a safety precaution to prevent air raids on the city. The leadership mandated that rule. There is no forgiveness for violation of that regulation.

I recall when some weeks ago I turned on the light switch in the bedroom. I had forgotten to check whether the shades had been pulled. Mother saw the lights on with the open shades. She was next to me in an instant, one hand on the switch, one on my face. Mother's scorn tasted bitter in my mouth. I wanted to scream at Hitler: Stop this war, stop it!

As we finish the supper dishes, the doorbell rings, taking us by surprise. Our hearts leap, who could be at the door? It is almost seven o'clock.

A man in the brown party uniform notifies us to leave the apartment by 8 o'clock next morning. "Bring food to last you for three weeks. There is no public transportation. Head for the western end of town. You will find vehicles assigned to carry you."

Before we comprehend he is gone. Just the echo of his footsteps throbbing in our throats. Apprehension seizes us. All color has drained from Mother. I have never seen her look so pale yellow. She struggles with the bad message.

"Liars! Traitors! Damned Nazis!" She explodes. "Annemie, we have to leave. We will be back in three weeks. We will be reunited with Papa; the war will be over. Life will return to normal." How does she know? I think. She is so desperate.

Suddenly a determined Mother puts her anger into action. She begins planning.

"Tomorrow is Monday, January 29, 1945," she declares. "It is cold. It has been minus 29 degrees today and no warmer tomorrow. We shall wear our warmest clothes. Let us try them right now."

I start with double underwear, two shirts and one woolen

pair of home-knit panties with legs down to the knees. Two pairs of high wool stockings and a warm full fleece slip. Then I put on a wool skirt and a wool sweater. I am 15 years old now and I don't always agree with Mother's tastes. But I know this is no time to argue. The winter coat just barely buttons.

Mother armors herself likewise. We both own a pair of leather boots. Scarves and the two warmest mittens are laid out. "This is what we are going to wear tomorrow!" Announces Mother.

"Now let's get suitcases. Two for you, Annemie, and I will pack two for myself."

My parents have nice possessions besides their beautiful furnishings. The crystal ware is lovely. We even have our own monogrammed red lead crystal glasses. Mother owns delicate Dresden china. She also has silverware with gold-coated handles.

"This is what I am going to pack," she thinks out loud, reaching for the silverware. "That has value and we can always trade it for food." Then she thinks of the cigarettes she has accumulated from when she worked at the Hospital. They are an excellent black-market item.

Back when Papa used to come on furlough, cigarettes were always traded for coffee beans. What a ceremony it was when Papa roasted the coffee beans in a pan on top of the stove. Ah, that aroma! And I even got to grind the beans. With the coffee mill held between my legs, I could inhale all that good smell.

"This suitcase will be used for food," I hear Mother say. "What can we pack? What do we have? Ha, bring food for three weeks, the Bonze (Bigwig) said. There is not enough food for three days in the house."

Gradually I realize what is happening. Tomorrow we will be on the road. Where will we be? We cannot even come home to our bed. Where will we sleep? I don't really want to go. I don't understand.

"Mother, do we have to go? I don't want to." Tears and sobs just come. Mother pulls me on the couch, close. We are too choked up to talk. I feel so miserable. I'd rather the world came to an end. I don't want to face tomorrow. I don't even want to listen to Mother. But she looks straight at me. "Annemie, we are leaving early in the morning while we have a chance. I am not exposing you to the Russian soldiers. Terrible things happen to teenagers and women. We could be killed. We have no choice."

"Mother, how do we make it to the opposite end of town? It must be 5 kilometers or so!"

"We will worry about it tomorrow. Let us throw two pillows into one suitcase. The featherbed is too heavy to carry. We have not packed the food yet. Let's bring all the bread we have. There is a pack of cheese. There is a little chunk of ham and the bag of oatmeal. Maybe we can even cook somewhere. And here is some Zwieback. A small can of fish is left still. The carrots – no, they will freeze. The wheat pasta might come in handy. The bouillon cubes too. And that is all the food that is left in the house. We should bring a sharp knife and a cup and a plate."

Mother jumps around like a wind-up toy. How can she keep her thoughts together? I feel like I am all knotted up and my body has to be forced into action.

"Annemie, let's use the last suitcase for extra clothes. Bring your warm pajamas and two towels." We look through our wardrobe and grab a few more things. Mother even throws in a few photos. A few important papers, birth certificates and such are added too.

The suitcases are closed and placed into the hallway. It's getting very late. Then one more walk through the apartment to make sure everything is all right. The shades are all pulled. The doors are all closed. I don't know why. Mother mentions that she will turn off the water in the morning so that the pipes won't freeze. "Everything will be fine when we come back," she says.

In bed, I bury myself under the covers. I don't want to hear or think. Those wagon treks appear in my mind. At least those people had their own wagon wheels from home. I can't imagine how our journey will go tomorrow. Journey? Oh, maybe there will be excitement. How dull life has been until now. Nothing ever happened. Dances were not allowed. There were no sports events. All the nice young men had become fighting soldiers or dead heroes. All boys 15 years or older had to avail themselves for the defense of the Vaterland. How can the Fuehrer hold such authority over millions of people? How did they all fall for him? I could sense that my parents never had sincere enthusiasm for the Nazis, nor did I. There never was any fun under their rule. How long has it been since I went to a movie theater with my good friend Gisela? I wonder where she is right now? It would be more comforting to have her and her family with us tomorrow. Mother said we have to leave. Maybe it won't even be so bad. Maybe . . .

Sounds like the doorbell. Oh, I must have been dreaming. Mother gets up. That's what it is, the alarm clock. "Let's bring the alarm clock, too," Mother mumbles.

Oh, my God, this is the day we have to leave home. Mother forces me to eat two slices of bread with jam and hot tea that she had saved for breakfast.

After all the layers of clothes on me, I must look like a big balloon. I can barely move! Mother shows me where she is hiding all the keys. "All the closets, desk drawers, and cabinets are locked," she says," so nobody can steal anything in case of a break in." Only the front door key is carefully tucked into her purse. "We will be back in three weeks," her goodbye words echo.

The suitcases are already heavy to drag down the stairs. "There is no way we can carry them for a long time, Mother." "Maybe we can fetch a ride with somebody or something," is her comment.

We more drag than carry the baggage. But that does not last for long. It's too heavy. We try to push the pieces through the snow. We discover that we cannot do that for long either.

Way ahead we see some moving figures. The first sign of

life. "That looks like a sled down the block," I say. "Run and see, Annemie," says Mother.

I return with a long sled. We are exuberant. The suitcases fit nicely on it, but they keep falling off. Mother decides to go back home for some rope.

The cold wind hits my face. I cover it more with my scarf. This 29th day of January is one of the coldest winter days. Yesterday the thermometer on the balcony read minus 34 degrees Celsius. With all the layers of clothes, my body is insulated and the cold cannot penetrate.

The rope is long enough to tie the suitcases and sled into one bundle. It holds together. The snow is more compacted in the street. It makes pulling the load easier. It is difficult to make it up and down the curb anyhow. We have not met a single vehicle.

There is no talk, just pulling the rope. We haul, and we lift the sled just like a pair of oxen pulling the plow through a muddy field. An enormous amount of energy seems to emanate from our bodies. We just have to make it to our destination. At least we are going with the wind. We have been dragging and pulling for more than an hour already. Some people are on the other side of the street. We are much too wrapped up in ourselves to pay attention to others. All we want to see is transportation for us. I wonder if we will have the strength to continue for another three hours maybe? We are getting very weary. But we keep moving ahead, our load still intact.

"Mother let's try to stop the car that's coming from behind us." But it does not even slow down. More people are headed the same direction we are going. They carry bags and suitcases, too. "I hope it isn't much further, Mother. I am tired." "Let's go for a while longer, and then we will take a rest," is the reply. This has already become an endurance test. What if ... what if ... No, I must not allow myself to think that way. Mother is very quiet. I used to think of her as somewhat of a complainer. But now I have certainly taken on that role.

The tall apartment buildings that lined the street until now are replaced by single-family dwellings.

"Annemie, we are in the western suburbs. Look ahead, there is some activity. It is some distance away. It looks like a bunch of trucks to me." "I wish they could come and pick us up, Mother."
Memories flash through my mind. I think of the time when we owned a car. I wish so badly I could be cozy and warm on the backseat cuddling under a blanket right now. Even without a brother or sister, I have never been lonely.

Oops! I almost drag Mother down with me. I don't know what made me fall. I shouldn't daydream!

We are passing a Konditorei (bakery). There is no life inside or outside. How I would love to stop for my favorite dessert, a cream puff and a cup of hot chocolate.

Sheer exhaustion makes it no longer enables us to carry our baggage. One by one the suitcases are left behind. The value of our possessions suddenly loses importance. Escaping the Russian tormenters becomes our main mission.

At last, we could see the open area. Four big and open trucks are overloaded with people. One vehicle is leaving. Another one is taking off. The drivers on the trucks don't think there will be more transportation. They are anxious to take off. Both remaining trucks are equally packed with people. There would not have been room for our suitcases that we abandoned. Panic grips us. Climbing up over the railing almost seems impossible. People extend their hands and pull us up. The gap in the middle of the truck box is tiny. I have to unbutton my coat, so I am flexible enough to sit down. There is no leg room. People who sit on the benches lean on the railing that surrounds the box. Mother and I are cramped. But we do not feel the icy wind. Our suitcases are gone for good. All our silverware will not buy us food. Will it do any one else any good? Our personal papers are lost. How can we live without IDs in Germany?

"Are you alright, Mother?" A slight nod with tears flowing uncontrollably down her cheeks is the answer. This is the first time since last night Mother is letting go of her feelings. Here we sit side-by-side with strangers; strangers instantly becoming refugee companions.

Only the sky above is visible to us. We are crowded in. It is impossible even to move a muscle. Truck horns blare. The driver yells that he is leaving now.

Nobody seems to know the destination of this caravan. The wheels start turning. All the bumps mold our shoulders together and bob us up as though we are all one body. Are we going to the same place the endless wagon trains we watched the other day were headed? Maybe they are better off. At least they got there first.

My eyelids won't stay open. I don't know how much time has elapsed when they open again. It is the sharp jolt that woke me. We must have hit something. People say that everything ahead of us has come to a stop. How badly we want to stretch our legs and arms. The driver warns us not to leave the vehicle. There is no guarantee we would get back on.

Faintly a baby's cry can be heard. Nobody talks. No one can move. People say that we who are packed down in the middle of the box at least don't have to experience the threat of the chilling winds.

Eventually, we move on slowly. Bump, bump, bump it goes. I hope we get to where we are going pretty soon. I am desperate for a bathroom. Every bump adds a higher degree of discomfort.

What is happening now? The cry of a piercing and hysterical voice is reaching us. It takes time before word of the ghastly happening reaches us. When the mother had tried to empty her baby's filled diaper, the flesh also tore. The baby did not react. The mother shouts, "My baby is dead."

The looks I exchange with Mother express so much sorrow and worry. Mother's eyes look so red. She weeps quietly.

This caravan creeps on what seems like an eternity. The people who form the outside row on the box are worse off than we are. Squashed as we are in the middle, at least we keep warm.

We are still in our home province of Silesia. Older women dress in their wide and long wool skirts. The blouses are covered by a loose fitting longer jacket. The huge, square scarf is folded in half and wraps around the head. The shoulders are draped by it also. It reaches all the way down to the waist which is adorned by its fringes. Black is the usual color for older people. Only the daring ones choose the deep blues or browns. Of course, the fabric is wool. But more than warm clothes are needed for this cruel expedition.

Dusk is settling in and we are still moving. Stops interrupt the slow going. I am getting cold. I feel like my inside is shivering. This is how it must feel on a ship. We seem to be swaying forward and backward and sideways.

Some commotion is stirring the crowd. Whispers stir the crowds. No one can move. But one can almost sense uneasy shifting among the people. Oh, I hope this signals the arrival at our destination. It is so uncomfortable being like a tightly rolled ball of cotton thread. It feels like we are moving very slowly.

Why does Mother act so strangely? She really seems bothered. Her finger is on her lips. She thinks she can hush the whispers. Horror shows in her eyes.

So that is why. An old woman has been tossed over the railing, her body lifeless and stiff. She froze to death. The pickup stops. The driver gets out and moves the body into the ditch alongside the road and covers it with snow. That's what people were whispering about.

We cannot see. We cannot move. I just want to get out of here. I don't care whether I am dead or alive. It is like I have no feeling, no emotion. People around me are just caged objects. How long have we been on here? It is nighttime. The moon is shining brightly.

Oh God, please do something, I plead. I want to go home. I am so tired of this. I am tired. Let me sleep and wake up when this is all over.

"Wake up, Annemie. We are there." "I want to sleep," I mumble. It takes a while to find myself. "What is going on?

Where are we, Mother?"

The driver announces that we will continue by train. We don't catch the name of the railroad station. It is a painful process to straighten up and move. It is early morning. I help Mother to get down. I have a hard time myself. My most immediate need right now is to relieve myself. I don't care where. Just a few steps over. Everybody is doing it.

The big clock hangs under the roof which stretches over the platform. There are only two tracks. It is past 7:20 AM. Customarily there are schedules of train arrivals and departures. They surely don't mean anything now. The station building is a red brick structure.

"Let's hurry toward the building." Mother holds unto my hand. The only thing we have is each other. People are all occupied with themselves and their own thoughts.

The building is filling up fast. At least it offers protection from the cold and the wind. The station master is somewhere but cannot offer when or whether the next train will arrive.

It is getting very crowded in here. At least we can move our feet and hands. Word trickles down that there is a faucet in the far corner. It will take a long time before it is our turn for a drink of water. We are thirsty, and we are hungry. We are also very afraid.

How will we go on from here? Where to? When will a train come by?

Some Hitler Jugend girls can be seen. They have sandwiches. Two slices of solid rye bread with a slice of cheese in between. And they have an aluminum cup with hot tea. The crowd of people is sectioned off and the food distributed to each person.

Nightfall is upon us once more. A whole day has gone by. People are afraid to miss a train while waiting inside the building. Most everybody is stepping outside. Mother and I share in that fear also. So, we line the track. It is so cold. The wind is howling a depressing tune.

No matter how far we stretch our heads in hope of

catching the sight of an oncoming train, there is no indication of any activity.

It seems like we have been waiting forever. The cold becomes unbearable. "Wouldn't a hot cup of tea or cocoa be so good right now, Mother? And even just a slice of dry bread with it? I am hungry."

"Ja, if only a train would come and take us to wherever we are going." The cold sends people back into the building. The temperature is minus 19 degrees Celsius.

"Let's go inside too, Annemie." My fingers and feet hurt from the cold and long waiting outside.

In spite of all the people, it is quiet in the building. Mother and I lean against the wall. Exhaustion takes over. We slide down and rest our heads on our knees.

"You take a nap, Annemie. I will stay awake and keep my ears open. We cannot both go to sleep and miss a train." We take turns napping. Time passes. Five minutes? Five hours? I don't know the difference.

It is growing light outside. A few people are always guarding the tracks. They are raising their heads in one direction. Are they hearing something? They motion us to come. The crowds move quickly. We are afraid to raise our hopes. But outside we really hear the rumbling sounds of an approaching train. Hurray! We are overjoyed.

"I hope we can get on, Mother. I hope there is enough room!" Our happiness immediately turns into disappointment. The railroad cars have so many people piled behind each window. We search for a door. It does not open. It is locked from the inside. And so is the next one. A window opens here and there. We learn that doors are locked for protection. Passengers are so crowded in, that the doors have to remain locked to hold them all in. Some people lift their small children through the windows. They try to climb in after them. The train starts rolling. The mothers do not make it. They are hysterical. Our hearts sink. Their kids are on the train riding off into the distance. Their mothers are left behind. So are we.

We cling to rumors of more trains to follow. But fear is overtaking us. The crowds are in a frenzy. The mothers are crying and praying out loud for their children. What can we do but wait?

The clattering of another train is heard in the distance. Everybody lines the tracks dangerously close. But this train does not even slow down. It just speeds by. Nobody leaves their spot. We stay where we are, hoping for another train to come and stop for us. We nervously wait.

I wonder about the future. What will it be? Will there be suffering? Will we make it? Will we fall to the enemy? And where are we going? Will we ever be home again? How long have we been gone from home?

The Sundays with Mother and Papa flash through my mind. They were such good times. They belonged just to the three of us. Where is Papa now? Will we see him soon? Will our family survive all this? How much fun it was to go on walks together. I loved the evenings when we sat around the radio and listened to a good suspense or adventure story.

Adventure? Is this an adventure we are experiencing now? No, this is a nightmare. A nightmare with no end in sight. Anger rages within me. Why is this happening to us? What have we done wrong? My family never believed in Nazism. My parents have never belonged to the Party. I remember Papa saying once that he can never expect a promotion without joining the Nazi Party. Sure, I had to join the Hitler Jugend, or else.

These bitter thoughts are still flashing through my mind. "Annemie, do you hear the dull noise in the distance?" "Yes, Mother, I do." The noise grows louder and soon a train comes into view. Fear overtakes joy. Will we get on this time? The train again is not even slowing down. It speeds right by.

We are informed that another train will shortly arrive. It does stop. People are pouring in. We are one of the first ones to board.

"Mother, sit down quick, there is one empty seat. A soldier

gives up his seat next to Mother. People and more people are piling in. They are on top of us. The windows are entirely blocked, and the daylight is obscured. It doesn't matter. At least there is hope, even though I am not sure for what. But we begin to move. The air is so stale. There is almost not enough room to breathe. I feel drained.

"I am going to sleep, Mother." No answer. Mother has already dozed off. It's dark now.

Dawn is breaking when I wake up. I want to stretch so badly. I am full of growing pains. But there is no room to shift at all. The wooden bench is hard and feels like it is grinding against the bones. But much worse than that, my bowels want to move. "Mother, I have to go to the bathroom. I cannot stand it much longer. I am miserable. My whole midsection feels like a big balloon. I am going to blow up." Mother pleads with the crowd to let me get by into the bathroom. People try to move. It is not possible.

I am worried. How will I survive this? I hurt everywhere. I wish I could explode and it would be all over. The pain sharpens. "Help me, Mother." There is no way. Somehow, I must have fallen back to sleep.

The train has stopped. The doors open. When the compartment is empty I slowly start to get up. I head for the restroom. Dear God, thank you, I pray.

***

We are in a town by the name of Goerlitz. I remember Goerlitz from geography class. It is pretty much straight west of Breslau. Maybe it is some 120 or more kilometers. We spot a few "Browncoats". Those party members are dividing us into groups. Everybody is assigned to a certain family. We are loaded onto a horse-drawn wagon. We are to be at our destination in half an hour or so.

Our new home is a beautiful estate in the country. There are no close neighbors. The brick building is majestic with stately trees in the yard.

A younger woman greets us formally and shows us to our

room. We can sense her indifference to us.

What a sight we must be. We are exhausted. Who would want to look at somebody so dirty and unkempt?

The two flights of stairs lead to a small, immaculate room. Two single beds, one small table with two chairs and a wardrobe don't allow for much extra room.

"I am Frau Hartwig. Your meals will be brought to your room. You will find the bathroom right off the hallway next to your room. You will share it with the maids." Mother hardly has time to thank Mrs. Hartwig before she disappears down the stairs.

I am touching the bed. It is a real bed. I cannot resist it. Immediately I stretch out on it. "Annemie, you are not going to sleep like this. Go to the bathroom and clean up first." I know I cannot change Mother's mind, so I might as well give in. The water in the bathroom is a thirst quencher.

Five minutes later I drop into bed, too weary to think or even dream.

A knock on the door awakens me. Where am I? Mother is reaching for her coat.

A servant informs us that the breakfast tray is on the table in the hallway. We may return it there after we are finished. She disappears as fast as she came.

Mother sets the tray on our table. She hands me my portion of oatmeal and a hard roll. We also have a cup of barley coffee. "Thank you, Mother. Isn't this deluxe? Breakfast in bed?" I indulge myself.

Mother eats at the table. "Maybe we will stay here until we can go home again." She shrugs her shoulders. The pain of the past days lingers.

What next? The possibility of being home soon is diminishing by the day. "On top of that we are being reduced to second-class citizens," expresses Mother. Then she continues, "We have not chosen to be here. We are not very welcome. I guess we should get acquainted with this place. This attic room has to be part of the servant quarters."

The world outside is covered with one vast white blanket. "These look like endless fields to me. They are probably wheat and rye producing." I add, "No wonder this building is so big. It must take many people to run this operation."

We put our smelly clothes back on. We want to explore our new environment. Maybe we can get hold of some laundry soap and ask permission to do some hand laundering in the bathroom.

It is a narrow staircase to the second floor. One young woman in a grey dress and a white apron is cleaning in one of the bedrooms.

Mother's "Good morning" catches her attention. "Are you looking for something?" she asks, barely interrupting her work. "Could I talk to the lady of the house?" questions Mother. "When Waltraud brings your dinner at noon, she will let you know," says the woman. With that, she proceeds with her cleaning.

We walk down the hall. The maroon floral carpet on the wide stairway to the main floor continues in the entrance hall. The ceilings are high, and the upper panes are mosaic. How stately! The veranda faces a big yard. All the doors off the hallway are closed. It is quiet. There is no sign of anyone's presence. We peek outside. It is windy and cold.

Upon returning to our room we know that we are expected to dwell separately from this wealthy family. They were asked to accommodate us. They welcome us no more than we want to be here.

When Waltraud brings the dinner tray she lets us know that Frau Hartwig can see us at 14:30 in the drawing room.

During a very businesslike meeting, Frau Hartwig wants to know whether our family name "Guderian" indicates a relationship to the Colonel General Heinz Guderian. After Mother's acknowledgment, she seems to carry on in a less arrogant manner. She says that she has confidential news that our stay will be of short duration. They already have to prepare Officer's Quarters. The house will be filled to capacity.

For the promise of some laundry soap and her hospitality, Mother thanks Frau Hartwig. She wishes us well and walks us to the hall.

I feel like I don't have enough energy to walk the steps back to our room. Mother is also dragging. The worry about the uncertain tomorrows leaves us totally drained. That means that the Russians have advanced some more. The lump in the stomach is suddenly there. We desperately want to go home again. But instead, the distance to home is increasing. We are so helpless. We just have to wait around until somebody comes along and tells us where to go and how to go. Maybe next time it will be a Russian soldier pointing a gun at us. This confinement is becoming more and more depressing. We cannot leave. Who knows how far the next stop from here is. The more time passes the unhappier we become. The evening meal hardly goes down. The dry bread is hard and coarse. The soup is watery cream of wheat.

The next day we spend anxiously waiting for some bad news. We have no radio, nothing to read, nothing to do but worry.

"I wonder where Papa is. Is he alive still in all this chaos?" I hear Mother say. She just sits and stares out the window.

When Waltraud brings dinner, she has some instructions for us. Tomorrow we will be returned to the railroad station. She has no further news.

Back on the horse-drawn wagon, the driver brings us to the railroad station the next morning. He does not say more than "Guten Tag" and "Auf Wiedersehen."

This time things run a little smoother. A train is being provided just for us refugees. Nobody tells us about our exact destination.

***

We arrive at a small town by the name of Koswig, some 35 kilometers northeast of Dresden. Now we have left Silesia behind. I guess that we are at least some 70 kilometers west of Goerlitz. Dresden is the capital of the province of Saxonia.

Dresden is well known for the arts. It has many museums and a well-recognized opera house. My parent's delicate china set had the "Dresden" stamp on the back of each piece.

A short bus ride brings us to a small house at the edge of town. An elderly woman is opening the door. She is understanding of our condition and apologizes for the plain and cold room. Frau Schramm is a widow. She is frail looking and must be in her late sixties. "You make yourself at home," she says. "Just let me know whether you need something. You will find me in the kitchen most of the time, the only warm place. If you need water and if you want to wash yourselves, you can do that in the kitchen. I always keep a big kettle with water on the stove. The toilet is also on the other side of the kitchen. The tea kettle has enough water for all of us. I don't really have much food in the house. But if you are hungry I can offer a slice of bread and there is some jam."

Frau Schramm's kindness is overwhelming, and Mother is almost too choked up to thank her.

Frau Schramm has no family. "I lost my husband six years ago, just before the war started in September 1939. He worked in a chemical plant in Dresden. He used to ride the train every day to the City. He put in long hours. He worked hard."

"Dresden is such a beautiful city. You should see the former King's castle. You have never seen anything like it. And the churches are so sacred with all the pretty and golden statutes. Are you Catholic or Lutheran?" she asks.

"We are Catholic," Mother answers almost hesitantly. The province of Saxony is predominantly Lutheran. The two ruling religions are Lutheran and Catholic, with twice as many Lutherans throughout the Country. Mother is afraid to create discord. I remember how I ran into some feuds with my friends in school over religion. At my last school days in Breslau, everybody confessed externally to atheism. That was Hitler's expectation and surely helped one's standing in the Nazi crowd. "There is only one Lutheran church in town," Frau Schramm points out. "These days we are hardly allowed to pray openly anyway."

"Isn't it a shame what is happening in Dresden," she continues. "The air raids have just been terrible. The British have been dropping their bombs all month like there is no tomorrow. And the poor people, ja, the poor people. They are trying to evacuate the people to the country. But they cannot get them out fast enough. Besides, there is no room anymore. The refugees are filling up every house there is. The whole situation is just unbelievably bad."

"This is the most news we have heard since we left home," Mother replies. "Annemie, we left home on January 29th, didn't we?" "Yes, Mother, it was on a Friday. What is the date today?" "Today is Thursday, the 8th of February 1945," states Frau Schramm.

Later on, in our room, we ponder our fate. We have has lost direction. We wish the last ten days were nonexistent. Do we even want to remember? Is this really happening to us? Why? Thank you, God, for nights. Don't make me think anymore. Don't let any more happen to us, please. Let us go home . . .

The next morning Frau Schramm tries her best to acquaint us with the small town. "I am not good on my feet," she says. She hands us a stamp from her rationing card and asks us to bring her a loaf of bread. "And stop at the mayor's office in town for a proof of your refugee status. With your refugee card you can probably buy as much, or as little, food as I can get," she adds.

Frau Schramm's acceptance of us makes us feel more like welcome guests than unwanted intruders.

The prospect of buying food ignites hope again! The happenings of the recent past cannot spoil today! "We are on a shopping spree." We explore a new town!

After a long walk into town, Mother exclaims, "See this long line of people ahead. It must be an indication of merchandise or something." "Let's buy anything there is, Mother."

"Sure," she answers. "And pay how? My cash is limited. I can't spend all the 500 Marks I have left." Both savings books are with local banks and of no value here. "If we can find a Post Office I will draw from the postal savings account." The money can be deposited or withdrawn at any Post Office throughout the country.

Way back, we used to go by train to Aunt Hedel's house. Aunt Hedel, Mother's younger sister, and my five cousins were fun to visit. We did a lot of fun stuff together and sometimes exchanged presents. Aunt Hedel always baked that good coffee cake with lots of poppy seed and streusel on top. She knew that it was my most favored. And she always stored lots of it under the bed in the cold bedroom.

The people are lined up in front of the bakery. We can hear both the Silesian and Saxonian dialects. They also speak High German. I am perplexed by the difference of dialects. Back in school, a history teacher was from Leipzig, the capital of Thueringen. Her brogue always intrigued me, even though she spoke "High German". That is the standard language taught in schools throughout Germany. An educated person speaks High German, my parents always stressed. I don't know the exact number of provinces, but there are at least some fifteen.

The two loaves of bread smell so good. Mother allows me to break the end piece off. I touch and smell it, and smell it some more before I revel in the taste of it. These breads, baked of coarse rye or barley, give the teeth a good workout. How good it tastes, even without lunch meat or cheese or fish.

Those good fish stores that had ample supply when we first moved to Breslau saw us at least every Friday. As Catholics, we were not allowed to eat meat on Friday, so Mother used to send me to the store with an empty bowl. The marinade was scooped into the dish along with the herring. The fried and then pickled herring came with good spicy liquid also. The smoked lochs were so delicious on a fresh and crisp hard roll at suppertime. Mother is a good cook. All sorts of her fried fish filets were always tasty. Friday was my favorite day when it came to meals.

Milk rice with browned butter and cinnamon sugar on top I also loved. I must be hungry, reminiscing about all the good food.

Next, we pass a little department store. We see underwear and stockings on the almost empty counters. We never dreamed of such finds. We can even buy one pair of each with our refugee pass. What great joy! Then we stop at the Post Office. The clerk behind the window counts 200 Mark. "Once every month you may draw 200 Mark," he says.

Before we head back home we find some carrots, potatoes and dried peas in a store. Frau Schramm is delighted with the goodies we spread on her kitchen table. "That will hold us for a few days. I have flour to thicken the soup. I have quite a bit of oatmeal left to last with the bread in the morning."

We know that Frau Schramm treats us like family. Nothing can interfere with my new home and family now. I rejoice. Wrapped in blankets we spend evenings near the kitchen stove. I play checkers with Frau Schramm. She outwits me, though, oftener than I like.

It is Tuesday evening, the 13th of February 1945. I am the official dishwasher and Frau Schramm insists she gets a clean apron for me. From her bedroom, she calls us to come quickly. The sky keeps lighting up in the distance.

I have never seen anything so strange. Is this a freak of nature? I think.

"Du lieber Gott (dear God)," says Frau Schramm, "they are bombing Dresden again." We all run outside to witness the spectacle in the sky. Quite often, outlines of what looks like Christmas trees appear high up in the sky and drop down. How bright they are. This show continues for about five minutes, illuminating the dark sky. Lots of "Christmas trees" keep falling from the sky.

"I have never seen the likes of it," says Frau Schramm. "Ach, those poor people. Dear God, help them, please don't make them suffer," she fades away as though in prayer. I stand in awe. I really can't quite apprehend the meaning of this show we became witness to. And it happened so close by.

Next morning the news on the radio is about the terror attack by the British on Dresden. The reports are conflicting. The number of people who perished is given by tens of thousands and even hundreds of thousands. The enemy has victimized helpless civilians. Women and children were burning like torches. In despair, they were seen jumping into the Elbe River. The railroad station was packed with thousands of refugees. The phosphorus bombs hit in the heart of downtown. They set the people on fire.

After all those announcements Frau Schramm folds her hands as though in prayer. First, she is speechless. But then she breaks the silence. She exclaims, "They are all the same, the British, the Americans, the Russians, the French and even our own Germans. How is this all going to end? Our whole home front is threatened and there is nothing we can do! Who thought the war would bring such deadly disaster? Anything is possible. Oh, Frau Guderian, what kind of world are we living in."

"I don't know either what is happening to our country," says Mother. "We have been driven away from our homes. The people in the big cities are being attacked by air. They have to die. Why? Who wanted this war? May Hitler and the Nazis be damned forever. Hitler turned the whole world against us. The Americans are so powerful! They and the Russians will probably wipe us from the map! Too bad they can't get Hitler and his SS. What the hell do we people have to do with it?"

Reality is looming over us again. I wonder how and when the end will come. The end of what? The war or us? I feel like I have lost my place in this world. I don't know where I belong anymore or if anyone wants us anymore.

Back home in Breslau, there was only one air raid that I can remember. Gisela was at my house then. When the sirens went off we ran outside to the balcony instead of to the basement. A Russian plane had dropped its bombs in one residential section. It happened within walking distance from home. So, we went to look at the damage. It was not a pretty sight. Some apartments were half erased. Dishes were on the table in one place, and the rest of the room was gone. Another apartment was gone except for one bed in the corner of the room. I think there were six fatalities.

So many big cities throughout the country were badly damaged by now. When my cousin Gerda from Koeln (Cologne) had stayed with us a short while in the spring of 1944, we learned what the air raids were like. She told us that at bedtime they never undressed. That way they were better prepared to leave the apartment when the sirens forewarned of an attack. They had five minutes to make it to the shelter. The chance of survival was much greater than in the basement of their apartment buildings. She said that the vibration could be felt all around them. And then when people left the shelter they were never sure what they would find. Often times, their houses or apartments were no longer there. So, friends and neighbors helped each other out until the Party made living arrangements for them. All the big cities in western Germany are suffering the same fate. The Americans are bombing the southwest of the country. The English are doing the same in the northwest area. How much easier it has become for me now to understand Gerda's account of the attacks.

Nothing changes in our day-to-day living. We wonder many a time whether our apartment in Breslau will be there for us when we can go home again. I try not to allow negative thoughts. They do, however, enter my mind. What if we can never go home? What if our home is gone? What if the Russians dominate us? What if …

The news we hear on the radio does not boost our morale. The Germans sustain heavy attacks on the Eastern Front, they tell us. Artillery fire is heavier again. Soviet attacks have failed. Only a few totally destroyed housing blocks had to be abandoned. On and on it goes. We don't have real facts until we get to witness them ourselves, like that fatal air raid on Dresden. Frau Schramm is coming down with a terrible cold. Mother takes over in the kitchen. Our diet consists of watery soups, legumes, and vegetables. Potatoes, barley, rye flour, an occasional pint of skim milk and even a quarter pound of margarine are allotted to us. Thank God we have kept healthy. I notice though, that Mother's emotional well-being is down. She seems depressed.

Already it is the last day of February. At today's shopping expedition we hear rumors that all refugees will be sent on.

A soldier, a native of the area, has returned home from the Eastern Front. His injuries left him unfit for further defense of the Deutsche Reich (German Homeland). The general consensus is that his news is much more trustworthy than what the news media is presenting. Mouth-to-mouth reports have it that German fighting men have fallen into Soviet hands by the thousands. Military events move so fast that it has become impossible to evacuate people in time. Serious damage has interrupted the transportation system.

Frau Schramm's reaction to all news rumors is very determined. "I will not leave my home under any circumstance," she says. "If I have to die here, so be it!" She no longer dwells on the subject.

This Tuesday is just as methodical as any other day. Mother and I are back from our shopping trip. We have some beef tallow, sauerkraut, and even three hard rye rolls to show for today's effort. Frau Schramm displays no interest in our goods.

"I have to tell you something. Sit down!" she orders. A minute or two elapses before she continues. "The Browncoat was here. He asked for you. You should stay home, he said. You will be moving on. You are to wait for further instructions."

My feelings go numb. That sickening weight settles in the stomach again. Mother's eyes are closed. Her face is white. She looks like a crumpled statue. It feels like darkness enveloping us. Nobody says anything. Nobody wants to talk. The remaining day is spent almost in silence. I don't know whether I want to be dead or alive.

Thursday morning, we have to say goodbye to Frau

Schramm with great sadness. It is not easy to find words. "May God be with you!" she says with an embrace. "And you, too!" is Mother's response.

The only visible train at the station is a long freight train. Some cars are filled. People are crowding around the railcar doors and filling the platform.

Hitler Jugend girls are handing out what looks like chunks of bread and are dishing out some soup to the people in the cars. Aluminum cups have become important possessions for refugees.

We stand in line and without too much delay we are entering a boxcar. We are piled in like cattle. The straw on the floor is meant for better seating. More and more people are still coming. Some faces look familiar. We have seen them in town. There are old men and both young and old women. Many children are with their mothers. It is getting terribly crowded. Mother and I are sitting on the floor, some two meters from the corner, our backs resting against the wall. They want to still fit more people in and for lack of space we have to pull our legs up. Next to Mother, a two- or three-year-old boy sits in his mother's lap. An old man sits right next to me. It looks like he is trying to sleep. Little kids are crying.

I feel nothing. I don't want to be part of this. I don't want to speak with anybody or even look at anyone. Of course, we don't know where we will be taken to. It is still winter. There is never any good news. Why would we even want to know what is going on? Why should anyone be concerned with our safety or well-being? All anybody cares about is destruction, killing, hurting … The Germans, the Russians, the Americans, the British, they are all the same. Now we are in a cattle train. Why should we feel like humans? As my thoughts go spinning, my body is emptied of all its energy.

A while later the doors are closed, and we hear the outside bars slammed into place. So now we are real prisoners. For what crime, I wonder.

There are four small openings near the ceiling that I can

see. They are secured by wire coverings. Maybe they are 30 centimeters or so. Gray light is filtering in and maybe enough air to keep us from suffocating. It surely stinks in here.

Next thing we feel is some motion. The rattle of the wheels drowns out the loudness in the car. They screech, they stop, they roll. The car sways, exerting pressure on us. We are pressed as tight together as we were on the pickup. We sway as one body with the motion of the train.

So, we are off to somewhere. The many bodies provide enough warmth. The many offensive body odors are also trapped in here. The constant moaning of a woman is getting to me. What a journey again! Isolated from the world! How long will we have to stay in here? Which direction are we going? How do we know we are not moving eastward? Will we even make it alive?

There is no sensation of the speed we are traveling at. We are rolling along, forever swaying. Left, right, left, right.

An old man's voice sounds weak and desperate. He says that he can hardly breathe. I, too, think it is hard to inhale this foul air.

Kids have to go to the bathroom. A tin can is being passed around and passed back to be emptied into a pail in the corner. I bury my nose into my hands. I faintly feel nauseous. Mother is not saying a word. It is still really hard to comprehend the happenings of the past few weeks. If only I could scream at someone or beat up someone. Whoever is the cause of all this misery.

I am so squashed. I cannot move at all. My heartbeat slows down. I feel like I am going numb.

The continued groaning of the wheels rises to a pitch and then abruptly stops. Soon the bars are lifted, and the doors slide open. Air, fresh air, is streaming in.

The word is that we are stopping for half an hour. People may get out to stretch and walk around. We have no idea where we are. The time is shortly after one o'clock. There is snow on the ground. Woods surround the train on either side. The crowds scatter in all directions. Some move awkwardly. Everybody is in search of their own tree to answer Mother Nature's call.

Within half an hour we resume our positions in our tomb. Hunger occupies us. The promise of food restores meaning to our being.

One hour passes. When the doors are opened again, Hitler Jugend groups scramble everywhere. We are to line up outside to receive the usual dry bread chunks. Soup is ladled into our aluminum cups. We are hungry enough not to mind drinking from the dirty cup.

"Where are we?" we shout in unison. "You are in Hof, Bavaria," comes the answer. "You are in the northeast corner of Bavaria." "How far are we from Dresden?" we ask. "Maybe some 140 kilometers southwest of there."

"I can hardly believe we are so far from home, Annemie. I don't know what God's plan is for us." It is difficult for Mother to accept the events of the past weeks. "We have to go on with life," she adds despairingly.

"It feels so good to stand up and stretch again, Mother." Everyone is searching for some privacy. More water is ladled into our cups upon request. In an almost amazing order, we climb back into our car. At least we are still being tended to. Hopefully, we will arrive at our destination soon. All we need is a temporary accommodation till we can go home, I reason with myself. Although deep in my heart I know there is Nobody Waiting.

On and on we roll again. Sometimes the train just stops. Other times it feels like we are switched to another track. It must be a bright moon. The open slot under the ceiling glows like a silvery light. Mother's head falls on my shoulder. She is asleep. I doze off.

When my eyes open I yell "no!" and close them quickly. I want to feast on my dream. The gate stands far open still. Instantly I am back in the meadow. The flowers widen my nostrils with their sweet smell. My chest doubles in size as I take the longest and deepest breath. Oh, it is so pretty here. The sun shines so bright. Each flower petal glows like a lamp. Somebody must have painted each blossom. Such brilliance! This whole field of flowers is drifting toward me. I don't even have to move. And the birds are worshipping the paradise. "What are you laughing about, Annemie?" Mother's voice. Why does she have to call me?

"Oh, Mother, I had the most beautiful dream." "You slept all night," she says. "Look through the ventilation hole above." The all blue opening shows daylight and a blue sky. I want to go back to my dream.

Regardless of my wish though, the boxcar becomes reality again. The air still stinks, kids are crying, old people are whimpering. I have to go to the bathroom. I am hungry and thirsty and my body aches. I want to stretch my legs so badly. I extend my arms. It helps me to inhale deeper. More doses of this stench are almost suffocating.

The train comes to a halt again. We are allowed to step outside. The usual routine of getting rid of our urgencies takes place along with stretching and moving around.

"You are in Pfarrkirchen, Bavaria" somebody's voice announces over a loudspeaker. "You are not far from your final destination. There is enough breakfast here for everyone. Please gather near your car to receive your food." A hard rye roll with jam and a cup of lukewarm barley coffee satisfy the immediate hunger.

While chewing, my mind wanders back to the pleasant breakfasts at home. In Breslau, early every weekday morning, Mother hung a clothes bag over the outside door handle. The bag was then filled with fresh, still warm Broetchen (continental rolls). The delivery man brought them from his bicycle-pulled trailer directly from the bakery's oven. Hmm, they were so crisp with fresh butter and my favorite plum jam. A hot cup of cocoa with it started the day off just right. Mother's good flour soup and even oatmeal do not sound so bad now.

It seems a long time before we start moving again. Finally,

we are in motion. We stop and go. Expectation and anxiety are mounting. What awaits us next?

The next stop brought us to the small town of Pfarrkirchen. Rolling hills stretched in the distance with snow on the ground and brown grass peeking through.

***

At the next stop, the bars were lifted, and the doors opened. A Browncoat welcomes us with the Nazi greeting of "Heil Hitler. I want this group to stay with me for placement to various homes."

We write our names and the number of people on his list. This takes a long time. I am freezing. We stand on the open platform. Only two boxcars are being emptied of people. The name of the village is Birnbach.

The house that comes into view behind the railroad station makes me think of many a fairytale Mother and Papa used to read to me. It is surrounded by tall pines, picturesquely nestled at the foot of a hill. The immaculately smooth, whitewashed color lends a stunning background to the ornate veranda built all around the second floor. The roof shingles are made of wood and stick out over the eves. Our roofs at home are all red tiles. The main carvings in the wooden balcony are all heart shaped. I am totally taken by the difference in building architecture compared to home. It looks like a different country to me.

Just what is happening to me, I wonder. When I think of home it is such a drab memory. It seems like houses, sidewalks and parks were all wrinkled at home. Somehow dense fog encumbers my thoughts.

"Frau Guderian, you have one daughter. We can send two people to the Brahms' place. There is still room for you two on the wagon over there," and he points to the wagon.

His dialect sounds like a foreign language. So, too, does the wagon driver's. He already points to the house we are assigned to. The small bridge we are crossing spans the Rot River. I can see two houses to the left. To the right, at a distance, a church steeple towers over what looks like a village situated on top of a hill.

The driver stops for us to get off in front of the white house. Then he continues without waiting.

"Do you think anyone has heard the knock on the door, Annemie?" asks Mother. I unsuccessfully search for a doorbell. We knock again. After that, a short, heavy, sort-of ruddy looking woman answers the door. Mother hands her the slip of paper from the Party man.

Wham, the door slams shut. Our throats tighten up. Despairing, Mother pounds on the door this time. The woman opens again. The message on the slip seems to have convinced her that it is her responsibility to give us accommodations.

"I didn't recognize you as the refugees. I have no say in what is going on. Things don't seem right to me. We have two empty bedrooms upstairs. I am taking you to the one with two beds." Reluctantly she leads us to the small room. The next moment she is gone. Shouting sounds come from the room next to ours. How hard it is to understand their dialect.

"Nice welcome, Mother, nice to meet her too, ha? She may not have any idea what is going on out there," I say to Mother. "Maybe she doesn't even know we are at war. We must be far away from the Russian front by now." Mother thinks the Russians are by far the worst enemy. The Americans landed in June of 1944 on Normandy beach in France. So maybe we are closer to that front now. How much longer can this last? I hope we can go home soon. Such thoughts sustain us. We have not even become acquainted with our new quarters yet.

"Doesn't that Bavarian dialect sound strange? Do you also feel like you have been dragged halfway around the world, Mother?" "Ja, and I wonder how long we will be intruders here this time. But somehow, we have to keep going, Annemie."

Heavy iron cross bars enclose the small window from the outside. "Look at the thickness of the walls, Mother." The village straight ahead looks like the one we saw from the railroad station. I can see no buildings between here and the village, just the gravel road. "And look at the almost white, wooden floorboards, Mother. The covers on the featherbeds are as white as ours at home." We each have our own hard chair and nothing to hang in the two-door wardrobe.

"First thing, let us find a toilet, Annemie." We bravely step outside our bedroom door. The wide hallway has the same wooden white floor. One door is opposite ours and another one is down the hall near the window. The wide steps end at the main floor which is red cobblestone. We discover four closed doors downstairs.

Mother this time timidly knocks at the one next to the stairs. The same woman opens. "Frau Brahms, where can we find the toilet?" "I am not Frau Brahms, I am Fraeulein (Miss) Brahms," she says. She looks goodly into her sixties. "This here is my brother." Herr (Mr.) Brahms barely looks up from the table. He acts like he wants to be left alone. He seems resentful of us. He must be at least seventy years old.

Fraeulein Brahms says, "We don't like to be disturbed when we are eating supper. But I will show you around." She takes us through the last door off the hallway into an expanding area. Straight ahead is the little room we are looking for. It looks like it was added to the building. At one side of this open area is a big and tall wooden door. "This is the barn," Fraeulein Brahms points out.

Wow, I have never seen a dwelling that houses both people and animals.

"What animals do you have, Fraeulein Brahms?" I ask. "We have two oxen, one cow, some pigs, and chickens. You see these wooden tubs," she continues. "We use them for washing clothes. If you want to wash yourselves, that's what they are for also. Come back to the kitchen and I will show you where you can always get warm water. But don't use too much."

Part of the big iron cook stove is a rectangular tub on top of one side. "I keep this filled with water all the time. So, it is always hot or at least lukewarm."

"I suppose I have to feed you too. If you have had nothing

to eat, you can fix yourselves a sandwich. The bread is in the pantry. The cheese is on the kitchen table and you can pour yourselves some milk." Mother thankfully accepts that offer while Fraeulein Brahms has her back turned toward us already. I get a glance of Mr. Brahms as he is walking into the adjoining room. He is tall, lean and almost bald. He looks quite wrinkly. He runs his shirt sleeve over his mustache.

Fraeulein Brahms offers us a seat at the table to eat our meal. Two long wooden deacon type benches are behind the table along each wall. No other furniture clutters the kitchen. Fraeulein Brahms bangs the dishpans on a heavy table in the pantry where the dishes are kept in a wooden cupboard. No one says a word. Do I relish the sandwich! So does Mother. Never have I eaten such good tasting bread! It is white, solid bread, sliced from a big round loaf. Why do people here in Bavaria have such good white bread, I ponder.

"Are you done, Annemie?" "Yes, Mother. That was so good."

"Thank you, Fraeulein Brahms, thank you very much." "Ja" she answers without looking our way.

In the hall downstairs I notice a wooden trough with a long-handled stomper resting in it. As I look I see a few leftover potatoes on the sides of the trough. I am not sure what it might be for.

"I think we might just have to go to bed dirty tonight," is Mother's comment. "No way do I feel like intruding Fraeulein Brahms' kitchen anymore tonight."

Moo, moo . . . where on earth am I? My eyes open slowly. This is not the ceiling of a barn. But it sure smells like one. Slowly my memory goes over yesterday's happenings. The night was the best part of it all. I pull the bedcover over my eyes and pretend I am at home.

It does not work though. My yearning wish of wanting to be home becomes a frustrated dream only. A vain hope for home takes up some room in my heart. It is so ugly to bring my thoughts from the world of imagination into the world of fact.

But the truth is that Mother and I are in Birnbach, Bavaria. Never before have I been that far from home. I didn't even know the world is so different. The little bit I have heard and seen here bears no resemblance to home. People talk a different German. How different the housing is. The Brahms make a living from farming. Unlike in Silesia, fields here surround the owner's house. At home farms form a circle. The living house is inhabited by people only. The other farm buildings are for the animals and the crops, feed, and seed. One or more shed-like buildings store the equipment and such. The smell of the big manure pile, oftentimes located in the center of the surrounding buildings, comes back to my mind. Here the barn shares our bedroom wall. It does smell a bit like barn in here.

"Annemie, are you awake?" "Yes, Mother." "Did you have a good night?" "I slept like a rock." Mother talks on. "I wonder what time it is. I hope it is not so late yet. I forgot to wind my wristwatch. Fraeulein Brahms will probably label us lazy if we come down after breakfast. I think she is determined to remain cool toward us. Can't you tell she does not want to give us a minute of her day? Our clothes need washing and so do we. Let us go down to the kitchen and hope that Fraeulein Brahms will brief us some more about living here."

Our knock on the kitchen door is answered by "come in here". The kitchen clock points to almost 9 o'clock. "We don't sleep this late in this house here. There is too much work to be done," she growls. But she offers us some home baked sweet rolls directly from a pan on top of the stove and a cup of coffee, substitute of course. Fraeulein Brahms assures us that her brother is gone this morning. It might be a good time to wash up in the wash-house, which is the open area between house and barn. Those little wooden tubs with two hollow grips are easy to handle but hard to clean after use. This cleansing of our bodies feels good in spite of the cold room. It is easy enough to mop up the cobblestone floor. I take the empty water pails out to the pump in front of the house and return them filled to the wash house. Quite obviously one pail is for drinking water. An aluminum ladle is draped over it.

A big keg, resting on a wooden stand draws our attention. The faucet-like handle must be for tapping. We really don't know what the contents are. "I am curious, Mother." I am holding the ladle underneath to see what comes out of this keg. Mother does not approve. But I try it anyway. Oh, before it shuts off it overflows and leaves a puddle on the floor. "It smells like wine," says Mother nervously. "Quick, Annemie, wipe the floor. If Fraeulein Brahms catches us stealing, she will throw us out immediately. I hurry. The leftover liquid in the ladle tastes sweet but also like alcohol. I don't think I will try that anymore. There sure is a big enough supply of it.

There is also a very big wooden table. The top is as bleached as the wooden floors in the house. It is at least seven meters long.

Back in the hallway, we meet Fraeulein Brahms. She points to the door opposite of the kitchen. "An old couple from Hamburg lives in these two rooms. They never come out," she adds. Then Fraeulein Brahms lets us know that every Friday she does her laundry. "Tomorrow after I am done, I will leave everything in the wash house and you can do your laundry. Ordinarily, I carry my clothes down to the River for rinsing. But it is still too cold now. Next month perhaps we can resume doing it. So now the rinsing water has to be carried in from the pump. "And be sure to leave everything clean," she says. Weird, I think. Sometimes I am in doubt whether I understand what she is saying. Her dialect is not easy to catch.

"Thank you so much, Fraeulein Brahms," I hear Mother say. Fraeulein Brahms is already walking away when Mother asks, "can you please give us some information about the village?" "Why don't you go there to find out for yourself," is Fraeulein Brahms snappy reply. Her impatience with us proves that she does not want to give us more of her time than she absolutely has to. We were forced upon her and definitely are intruders and an inconvenience.

The next day we decide to go to the village. Mother locks

and takes the key out of our door. I offer my opinion. "What needs to be under lock and key Mother?" She does not answer. Well, that is just her way.

From a distance, the Brahms' property looks like a painting. The small windows interrupt the gleaming white and smooth cement walls. All the iron bars across the windows probably are no interference since the panes open to the inside. The brown wooden shutters are so ornate, showing off the carved wooden hearts. Two big trees have outgrown the house. Only one close neighbor's property is visible. Expanding fields and meadows stretch from the house on two sides. A small path leads to the Rot River flowing only some 150 meters from the house.

To judge by the sun, we are walking north toward Birnbach. The two kilometers gravel road is lined with trees all the way. The walk is slightly uphill. Unlike the apartment buildings at home, these houses are so individual in character. Some show paintings on the outside. The style resembles mountain chalets, the kind one wants to cuddle inside by a warm fire and hope for lots of snow and wind blowing outside. On Main Street, two adjoining buildings advertise "Gasthaus mit Zimmer" (Inn with Rooms). Across the street is a bakery shop. We also spot a butcher shop.

At the bakery we are told to go to the Buergermeister (Mayor's Office), to receive our refugee identification. We run into more refugees here. How easily they are identified. Dirty clothes and sorrowful expressions give them away. We talk to some. We all share in the same fate. The girl standing next to me is named Renate. She is fifteen years old, just like I am. She has a nine-year-old brother, named Wolfgang. Her mother talks to mine. They are from Upper Silesia, just south of where we are from. Now they live in the neighboring small community of Untertattenbach.

Back in the bakery, we were lucky to get two hard rolls. "The doors open at 8 o'clock in the morning. You will find long lines by then already," we are told. At the butcher shop, we are able to buy two small sausages. We are overjoyed. How long has it been since we bought some food?

"Are you thirsty too, Annemie? If we could sit down at the Inn and get a glass of milk or even a Brause (soft drink), we could feast."

"Sure, Mother, let us do that." Just the thought of it makes me swallow repeatedly with anticipation.

As we enter the Inn, the waiter makes a dash at us immediately and asks in his dialect, "What do you wish?" Mother tugs on my coat and says, "Thank you, we are just taking a look at your lovely place. We will come back some other time."

The interior of the Inn much resembles the Brahms' kitchen. All along the walls, all the deacon benches display paintings of bright colors or carvings. The natural wood floors blend with the light-colored table tops. The stenciled border on the upper edge of the wall pulls the low ceiling down even more. The windows are small and have the iron bars.

"Annemie, we cannot afford such a treat." My mood slumps and Mother's is down. Everything we do, any undertaking reminds us of our status. We are banished. We don't belong.

We head back home. I try to think of another word for home. This is not home. I don't know what to call it. This is just sort of a hiding place.

My stomach makes loud noises as we are walking. "Mother, could I have a bite of the roll? I am so hungry." In no time both the roll and sausage are devoured. I am still hungry, but I must not ask for Mother's share.

Back at home Mother stretches out on the bed. She cries and cries. I am stretched out too. I have to listen to Mother's sobs. I hate myself. I hate the world.

I want to talk to somebody who is happy. Who? Dear God, why do you do this to us? What are you going to do next? What do you want me to do? Can't you make me feel better?

My thoughts return to Renate. I wish I could go to Untertattenbach and talk to her. Talk about school, talk about home. That would feel so good. I am going to look for her all over next time in Birnbach. I can hardly wait! I want to be happy!

Mother is asleep. I sneak out the door. I am going to explore this whole place. The barn door in the wash house is slightly open.

"Guten Tag, Herr Brahms," "Gruess Gott (Greet God)," he answers. Everybody here says Greet God in lieu of Good Day. He keeps pitching the manure from the pig stall onto the wheelbarrow. "This is a nice barn," I say. "Ja" is the most I can get out of him in spite of my continued efforts to make conversation. "Maybe I could help with something?" "Ja, maybe some time," he says. I am encouraged. In the washhouse I notice an empty pail of water. I fill it up at the pump.

At the other side of the house, a lot of firewood is stacked against the wall. I will offer to carry wood into the house, I decide. But for now, I better go back up before Mother worries about me.

"Mother, guess what I have done. I offered my help to Herr Brahms in the barn and he said, ja, maybe some time I can help. And I also filled the empty water pail in the wash house. Maybe the Brahms will even learn to like us in time." My enthusiasm does not have a courageous effect on Mother. "I just have a hard time adjusting to these people," she says.

Silesia to me means home and Bavaria is foreign, but not an enemy. All of Germany is fighting the enemy. Just where might the enemy be now? Didn't I hear some native Bavarians at the bakery talk about how the Americans "better not come closer"? Victory, victory! Those words still echo in my ears from the radio news. Somehow the atmosphere of war is not ever present on people's minds here.

"Maybe the Brahms will accept you more easily, Annemie. Do they expect pay from us? I cannot give away my last cash. I will need it when the time comes to travel home. I will have to talk to Fraeulein Brahms."

"We were ordered to accommodate you. We have to supply

shelter and food for you till the war is over." Fraeulein Brahms expresses with hostility to Mother's statement.

"Perhaps we can offer our help. My daughter Annemie likes to pitch in with any work. She likes to be outdoors. Just assign her to tasks."

"I like to do my own cooking and kitchen work. But you certainly can help to keep this place clean. With more people living here the house is apt to get dirtier. My brother likes a clean house. Every Saturday I scrub all the floors on my knees and wet mop the stone floors. You can do that, Frau Guderian, while I do the baking."

I notice Mother's gulping. She does not answer.

"Can I carry the firewood in, Fraeulein Brahms?" I ask.

"You can do that. First, you carry it in the washhouse from the outside and then the box by the kitchen stove should be kept full. Be sure you sweep up after each job."

Fraeulein Brahms continues, "Mostly we eat supper at 6 o'clock. Dinner is at 12:30 and breakfast around 8 o'clock after the morning chores. You can work on the wood supply right now, Annemie." This is the first time Miss Brahms calls me by my name. I explain to her that I own no other clothes than the ones I wore on my body when we had to leave home. She shakes her head like it makes no sense to her. "I guess I can find an apron for you," she replies walking away already.

Confidently I carry out my assigned duty. It makes me feel good. Fraeulein Brahms extends her sense of trust by letting me help her, I reason. She surely does not extend any trust towards Mother. But isn't Mother distancing herself somewhat? And now she is practically being ordered to scrub floors on her knees. At home she had a cleaning lady to sweep and wash the steps every other week when it was her turn in the apartment house. Our home sparkled with cleanliness always. But Mother never allowed herself to be seen in an apron. That was an indication of lowliness.

I don't care. It makes me feel great to work. It might just help us to move closer to the Brahms household, I think.

At the supper table, Fraeulein Brahms talks about Emma. She will be coming to help with the laundry. Emma lives two villages away. She comes to help out two or three days a week.

"How does she get here, Fraeulein Brahms?" I want to know. She explains, "She rides the bicycle. When the weather gets too bad, she has to walk. With all the snow gone already, the roads are good. The ground is still frozen, so there is no mud either."

"I could eat a whole loaf of this bread. Fraeulein Brahms, this is the best bread I have ever eaten in my whole life. Do you bake all your bread?"

"You be sure I do." "We only had rye or barley bread at home," I continue. "Where do you get the white flour?"

"We don't just go and buy it. We work hard all year long in the field. We exchange the wheat we grow for flour at the mill. What have you worked for?" She leans over the table as she speaks.

Mother pokes me under the table. I get her message, time for me to shut my mouth. "My husband is a civil servant. He became part of the Militaer (military) during the war. We have no idea of his whereabouts. We had a beautiful home and had to walk away from it with just the clothes on our backs. I hope the war ends soon and we can go home."

"I hope so too," says Fraeulein Brahms. This crisp talk across the supper table does not sound friendly to me.

Herr Brahms hardly ever speaks. "Could I help with the supper dishes, Fraeulein Brahms?" I ask. I will wash my own dishes, but you can dry them, Annemie."

"Thank you, good night." With that Mother goes back upstairs.

The following morning Mother and I eat breakfast alone. Fraeulein Brahms is already busy in the wash house. With her is Emma. We can't believe the procedure we witness. Each piece of wash is taken from the steaming wooden tub. It is then spread out on that big wooden table. With a most peculiar brush, it is scrubbed for a long time. The brush is repeatedly dipped into the suds in the tub.

"This here is Emma." "Greet God," Emma nods to us. "And these are the new people we had to put up," Fraeulein Brahms points to us. "If we had warm weather you could help carry this wash to the river and help us rinse it," babbles Emma while scrubbing away.

I keep wondering why so many things are done differently here.

I notice that Emma's throat has that big bulge just like Fraeulein Brahms', a big protruding lump. Strange! I think. I have noticed in town that other native women have that same big bulge protruding from their throats.

Emma is not a striking beauty. She has a broad face with reddish skin. She smiles with ease and there is a pleasant simplicity about her. She looks at least in her thirties to me.

"It will be afternoon before you can wash your things," comes Fraeulein Brahms' declaration. Mother is on her way back to the room while I stay around a bit and watch.

"I have never seen a brush like that," I admit. "Have you lived in Germany before?" Fraeulein Brahms uses her sharp tongue again. Emma explains that this brush is made from horse hair, from the tail. It makes the brush just right for scrubbing the bedding and table clothes and the rest of the clothes. Besides it is easy to hang on to.

Lots of water is used for rinsing. So, I am assigned to carry water in from the pump. I have a feeling that Emma takes to me. If for no other reason, I am easing her workload.

Pretty soon Fraeulein Brahms takes off for the kitchen to prepare dinner. The big meal customarily is eaten at noon time.

Without Fraeulein Brahms' presence, Emma becomes quite talkative. I have to listen closely to catch all her words. Her dialect seems more pronounced yet than the Brahms'. Emma talks about her home. She says, she lives in the hinterlands. Her father has a very small farm. Her Mother died a long time ago, and she has two younger sisters. One helps her father and the other one works at another place just like Emma does. "We don't have much money," she says.

"Do you have to pass through Untertattenbach on your way here, Emma?" "Yes, I do. It takes me about one hour to walk. On the bicycle, I can make it in less than half that time." She points in the direction to Untertattenbach. "It is across the pasture. You can see parts of it from here. I like to come here because it is not as boring as home. My girlfriend Liesel lives in the neighboring house here. Some Saturday's the Brahms let me stay overnight. Liesel and I walk to the railroad station. We like to watch people, especially boys when the train comes in. You can come with us some time."

Emma wants to hear about me. She has a hard time comprehending my background. "We hardly know that there is a war going on. It is hard to buy things at the store. We grow our own wheat and some vegetables. We butcher our own pig. We have enough to eat. Sometimes we need work clothes that we cannot afford. But we keep patching them. We cannot afford to buy much. And you own nothing?" she asks thoughtfully. "How can that be?" she adds.

I have heard some people say that the American troops are coming this way. I have not paid much attention to it. We don't have a radio. Sometimes the Brahms listen to theirs. I hardly ever do.

"Dinnertime!" calls Fraeulein Brahms. Mother comes. Mr. Brahms has already taken his place at the table. As always, I am awed by the table setting. I have been involved with it long enough to become more forgiving of this most different of all customs.

A slightly concave, thick wooden plate and silverware are placed on top of a white, coarsely spun linen tablecloth. In the center of the table is a brown earthen pot filled with Sauerkraut. A similar brown pot containing yogurt is placed between two place settings. There are no cups or glasses. A big jug sits on the table. Fraeulein Brahms makes good sized dumplings from the good white bread, flour, and eggs.

She takes each plate to the stove and puts a dumpling and

smoked pork on. She also ladles some of the liquid that the meat has been cooked in, over it. She then joins us and says a familiar table prayer, "Come o Jesus, be our guest ..." Now everybody reaches for their soup spoon and plunges it into the center pot for Sauerkraut. I watch as they repeat this procedure spoon by spoonful. I always had a strong dislike for sharing food with anyone, even my own family. "Eat," orders Fraeulein Brahms. I know I have no other choice. So, I hold my breath and reach for the Sauerkraut once. Ah, but the dumplings are plenty good.

"Such good tasting dumplings," I say. Emma responds with "Ja, Fraeulein Brahms knows how to make the best-tasting dumplings from her good bread." I savor each bite of the dumpling, dipped into that good broth. The smoked meat tastes really good, too.

Herr Brahms reaches for the big jug and takes a few sips. Saliva runs from both sides of his mouth. His mustache catches the drippings from his nose. Then he hands the jug on to Fraeulein Brahms. I am next. I do not have time to think how to get out of this one. I force myself to sample the contents. I am sure it comes from the big keg in the wash house. It does taste much more like wine than juice. I think of the holidays when Mother and Papa had always allowed me to have a small glass of wine. "Hmm, this tastes not so bad, what is it?" I ask. "Don't you know what most (cider) is?" Fraeulein Brahms wants to know. She must think the whole world lives like she does.

"This most is made from the wild pears that are growing everywhere. Many roads are lined with pear trees. They are very sweet. They taste best when fermented into most," clarifies Emma. Boy, I think, these people are getting their load of alcohol every day.

Thank God the brown yogurt pot is placed between Mother and me. It ought to be good. Fraeulein Brahms informs us how she poured milk six months ago into the earthenware. Then she stores it on a big shelf just halfway down to the cellar.

It has to be dark and just the right temperature. She keeps that big shelf full all the time. This same dinner is being served day after day after day.

At the end of the meal both the Brahms and Emma lick their silverware, wipe it on the edge of the tablecloth and back into the table drawer it goes. I can hardly believe it. "You don't," I blurt out. "Ouch!" I stammer. Mother steps so hard on my foot, it hurts.

What a ridiculous custom! I vowed to myself already that I will sneak into the kitchen alone and wash that silverware after every dinner. And if I have to, I'll do it in the middle of the night!

"You can fold up the tablecloth. It goes in the cabinet in the living room." This room is furnished just like the kitchen. Two of those deacon benches are alongside the walls. Only they are covered with brown cushions. Herr Brahms is stretched out on one of those by the window. With only the cabinet hugging the fourth wall, that white wooden floor seems to stretch a far distance.

Done helping with the kitchen chores, I stop by the washhouse to see how Emma is doing. She is busily wringing out her wash. "That bedding needs lots of water to get the soap out," she remarks. So, I supply her with more pails of water from the pump. "In a while, you can get busy with your clothes," she says.

Upstairs Mother and I gather the few pieces of clothing we own. When we come down Emma asks in disbelief, "Is that all you have?" Boy, does that underwear need scrubbing. I like doing this. This brush works swell on clothes spread all over the table. It is high enough, so I don't have to stoop down. I follow Emma out into the yard with my clean smelling clothes. I help her hang her load after mine is already fluttering on the line.

It is only three o'clock. Mother decides to walk to town. When entering Birnbach, I see so much I have missed before. All the buildings are so beautiful. I feel like I am looking at a picture book more than reality. Many houses are snow white.

Others are light pink, tawny brown and pale green. Carved verandas surround all the upper stories. Some balconies look so decorative with the bright paintings of flowers and heart borders. The small windows with their iron bars and carved shutters harmonize perfectly with the somewhat recessed and low entrance doors.

As the street curves, it takes on more of a business-like atmosphere. Above one window the sign reads Kraemer's Geschaeft (Business) and underneath Tools and Small Machines. Next to that is Hindl's Kaufhaus (Department Store).

"Let's go in and see what they have, Annemie." We enter with a "Greet God" after the chime of the doorbell.

"What are you looking for?" The lady asks in her dialect with great courtesy. "Our Store is not stocked very well, a result of the war. May I show you what we have?" She shows us some bath towels, some fabric, and some enamelware. And she points to some toys. She can only sell us one towel. Mother buys a few meters of that white fabric with black stripes. It is really a lining material of cheap rayon. But she figures she might be able to sew a dress and blouse from it. She even acquires a spool of thread.

A bit further down the Street is the Sparkasse (Bank). It is a local bank that does not recognize either of Mothers' saving books. Across the street, in the window, the sign reads Friedl – Lebensmittel (Groceries). There is a scarce supply of some goods, such as preserves, salt, pepper, barley coffee and such things. There are few cheeses and some margarine. "Milk supply exhausted for the day" reads the handwritten sign. Mother asks for a quarter pound of hard candy, displayed in a glass jar. The sales Lady asks if we have young children in the family. Since we don't, these sweets are off limits for us. Our rationing cards allow as little as nothing in the food department. Our accommodations are "with food included".

Down the block, a small sign on a narrow door points to the upstairs, Vittel's shoe repair. Mother looks at our feet and wonders how long our boots will hold out. Maybe the cobbler has some discarded shoes on hand. The old man looks over the rim of his glasses uttering "Greet God." He takes out the small nails from between his lips and gets up. In answer to Mother's question, he points to two rows of sandals he has made. They are all uniform with a rigid wooden wedge sole. Brown or black narrow leather strips are nailed to the wood. He kindly suggests measuring our feet. "I am quite busy, and the waiting time is six weeks," he says. "Oh, thank you. We will come back." "Do that," he answers. Of course, it is too late to go to the bakery. In fact, it is closed after four o'clock.

"Look, Mother, who is coming our way." It is Renate with her mother and her brother. I jump ahead to meet Renate and so does she. Mother visits with Frau Brunke. With a stick, Wolfgang draws outlines of houses on the ground. "You come to Birnbach often, Renate?" I want to know. "Almost every day," she says. We have so much to talk about. We compare our lives from our pre-refugee days. They are so similar. We both had attended high school. We were in tenth grade when the war abruptly cut off all our friends and brought our daily routine lives to an end.

"We have to move on, Annemie. Frau Brunke has invited us for a visit on Sunday afternoon." We all shake hands. Both Renate and I don't hide our joy of seeing each other soon. She will be a swell friend, I think to myself. I am more cheerful than I have been in a long time.

"Aren't you also surprised Mother, that Emma is not working tomorrow, Saturday?" "No, Fraeulein Brahms has a new maid now. I hope I can find all her dirt," Mother adds sarcastically. "I can't stand the thought of scrubbing for her. If I knew where to go, I would move on. How does Otto Reuter sing the hit? In Fuenfzig Jahren ist alles vorbei (in fifty years everything will be over with). I hope it will not last that long anymore!"

I feel sorry for Mother. "I will help you, Mother. On Sunday we get to go to the Brunke's place," I say, hoping to cheer her up.

On Saturday we are equipped with two pails of water, rags, scrub brushes, one with a long handle, and a wet mop. Mother and I divide the chores. General Brahms, as we think of her now, wants the upper as well as lower hall only damp mopped. She requires hand scrubbing of the stairs. The living room also needs scrubbing with the brush. So, Mother and I are in agreement that she starts scrubbing the upper hallway. I will take on the living room, working my way toward Mother's area. I prefer working on my knees. Fraeulein Brahms brings me some very fine, almost white sand. "This is for stubborn spots that won't come off easily. Just pour it on and scrub hard. You are doing a thorough job," she says, sounding almost pleased.

This work brings back memories of the time Mariele polished silverware with fine sand. I really wonder where she and her family might be. And I keep wondering about Gisela a lot. Who would ever have thought that we would become so separated from each other? Oh, it is best not to start thinking.

At least there is no clutter to be moved out of the way before starting to clean. Strangely, I get satisfaction from this work. Maybe I better not convey these thoughts to Mother. Next, I tackle the stairs while Mother is still working on the upper hallway. It seems like a whole kilometer from one end of the hallway to the other.

Downstairs the lady from Hamburg steps out of her door. She looks obese in her loose, long smock. On her head, she wears a ruffled white nightcap like Little Red Riding Hood's Grandmother. She empties her water pail outside. I bid her a "Greet God." Her "Good Morning" is hardly audible from behind the quickly closed door.

At the back of the stone floor hallway, only the trough needs working around. I found out what the potatoes in it are for. But I don't know whose job it is to stamp the steaming hot potatoes every morning. Some grain or table scraps are mixed in with it. This is the stuff that fattens up the pigs. And eventually, they end up on the wooden platter to delight our taste buds. "Hmm, does it smell good in here!" Noisily my nostrils take in that good bakery like smell. Saturday is "Dampfnudel (steam noodle) day. It is rewarding after all the hard work. I had never heard of Dampfnudel. They are cooking in that large pan with the wooden cover on top of the stove. I am glad dinnertime is not far away.

The dinner table is set as usual. The big jug waits in the middle of the table again and so does the sauerkraut pot. Fraeulein Brahms opens the pan right on top of the stove. Hot steam pours out and she quickly pulls away her face. "They have to be cooked airtight, or they cave in," she says. So that explains the name. The big pan is filled to the brim with these dumpling-like goodies. The bottom of each dumpling is very thick and so crunchy, crusty. The filling in the center is a thick prune sauce. "This is made of yeast dough and baked in a lot of butter and milk," explains Fraeulein Brahms. So, after the sauerkraut ritual, I devour two huge steam noodles. I pass the cider jug by and convince Fraeulein Brahms that I prefer not to drink with my meal.

Mother goes upstairs. "You can clean up the kitchen floor as soon as we are finished with the dishes, Annemie." "Sure, Fraeulein Brahms, first I will bring in more firewood so that I don't mess up the clean floor." I am highly pleased with my slyness, determining the next step.

At the supper table, Fraeulein Brahms tells us that Holy Mass is at 9:30 in the morning. "Come down at 7:30 for breakfast. The Lord made Sunday a special day. So, we start with a special meal," she announces. Herr Brahms wears a white shirt and tie. It does not make him more talkative or give more expression to his face. Fraeulein Brahms serves the barley coffee in a soup dish. Never before have I consumed coffee with a soup spoon. The next serving consists of soup also. Some of the daily "pig-potatoes" are sliced into some sort of sour cream soup. It takes getting used to. I don't understand what is so special about this meal. Maybe potatoes are a Sunday treat.

"You can find your way to church," Fraeulein Brahms

expresses. She absolutely does not want to be seen with us refugees.

Once in church, Mother and I head for one of the empty pews. The native people point to the name label for each seat. We sort of ignore it and feel there is room enough for two more. All the seats are not filled. Even in church, the refugees are not received kindly. All Bavarians are Catholics. Maybe someday somebody will push their faces in. I stop myself. The Lord won't tolerate such thoughts.

A narrow walking path winds through the pasture to Untertattenbach. Ten minutes later Renate and Wolfgang wave at us from a distance. They lead us to their abode. They have a tiny red brick house to themselves. It actually is the baking house. The main floor accommodates the baking oven. Renate says that lots of big loaves of bread and coffee cakes are baked here once a week. Upstairs Frau Brunke welcomes us to a tiny kitchen and a small bedroom.

There is so much to talk about, so much to say. While our mothers are exchanging their backgrounds and experiences, Renate and I go into the bedroom to talk. Our only audience is Wolfgang. We can't get over the similarity of our past. Oppeln, Renate's hometown is some 70 kilometers south of Breslau. The Oder River flows through both cities.

Renate says, she really likes high school. She talks a lot about a cousin of hers, who only went through eight school years. He already was in an apprenticeship program for carpentry. She says her uncle just worked in a sawmill. He was too poor to pay for his son's high school education. Renate thinks of becoming a nurse or even a doctor. We both took English class when we started high school at fifth grade. "Oh good," Renate blurts out, "now we can talk in English when we don't want Bubie to hear what we are saying." Renate calls her brother "Bubie". It is a common or affectionate form to call young boys and she points to her brother. "Don't be a wise guy," says Wolfgang sulkily. We do have fun though testing our English communication.

I let Renate know that languages were my favored subjects. I also took advantage of French and Spanish that were offered in my school. I do like the sound of different languages. My English teacher had sometimes sent me to a higher grade, just to read out loud to them. She had said that I pronounced my English so well. "I plan to be an interpreter or translator," I tell Renate.

Renate's and my pleading for a longer visit does not work. Mother is already thanking Frau Brunke for a wonderful afternoon. "I envy your independent housing. Come and see how we live." "Ja, thank you, Frau Guderian. We will do that some afternoon this week." With that, we are on our way back. "This was a great visit! I got rid of a lot of pent-up feelings. How did you like your talk with Renate and Wolfgang, Annemie?" "I liked it a lot, Mother. They are all so nice. Renate and I tried to even speak English with each other. Wolfgang did not like it, of course. I am happy that they are coming to see us, too."

One day when Emma is working, it is her job to make more firewood. With my help, she can use the longer saw with both handles. That makes her job a little easier and also saves her time. Boy, does she tackle those logs with the ax. She works just like a man. I pile the chopped wood. I would like to try chopping, but Emma would not even let me try. "That is too rough for you," she says. "Because of your help with piling the wood, I will be finished sooner than usual. That will give us some extra time for visiting."

The sun feels warm. April is here by now. We worked up a sweat. Emma is done with her job for today. She cups her hands for a drink of water while I pump. Then we sit down on the bench that rests against the house next to the entrance door. "I am staying over this Saturday night." "Do you sleep across from our bedroom, Emma, or is that Herr Brahms' room?" "Oh no, Herr and Fraeulein Brahms sleep in the room next to yours. The door across from you really has two rooms behind it. They don't use those. The old couple downstairs, from

Hamburg, have two rooms also. They have lived here for quite some time. Somebody comes and helps them often. They were brought here because of the air raids in Northern Germany. The Brahms' house is big.

"I sleep downstairs on the davenport." And then she almost whispers. "My boyfriend comes every other week, but the Brahms don't know it. He comes later at night. I let him in the front door. We are very quiet. And he leaves before morning. He is one year younger than I am. He is only 28 years old. You won't tell anyone about it, will you?" I assure her that I will not. I am not too comfortable with that information. I decide not to pass it on to Mother. I will just try to forget it. Or I could tell Renate, is my afterthought.

In the evening Emma invites me to come next door with her to visit her girlfriend Liesel. She is single also and lives with her mother. Liesel has a little girl, two years old. I have to listen very closely again to understand what they are saying to each other. Some words still sound strange. Emma and Liesel make plans for Sunday afternoon. They want to walk to Birnbach. Liesel comments on the many strange people in the village. Emma explains that they are just refugees. Liesel does not like their invasion. She makes it clear that she does not like those strangers. She says they think they are entitled to everything. They think they can empty the stores of the last merchandise. "They sure are disrupting our peace," she rattles on. She makes me feel ill at ease. I am glad when we are leaving. Emma tells me that many girls have babies already. "They do it everywhere, in the barn, in the hayfield," she whispers. "But they are all Catholics?" I ask. "That does not have anything to do with it," she says. To be honest, I don't quite understand.

This is already the third week in April. Recently it has been raining quite a bit. Mother spends many hours almost motionless. She does not leave our room more than she has to. When she talks she recounts the days with Papa at home, the good times, before the Nazi years. She is always looking back. One part of my mind is engaged with home and the other is concerned with life in the new surroundings. I don't want to continuously grieve over the happenings of the past few months. But there is uncertainty, an ever-present fear of the future. Renate's friendship makes my days so much more bearable. Almost every day after supper we meet halfway across the pasture. We laugh at each other's appearance. The same boots, same outfit every day. We try to imitate the native dialect. We are surprised at our success with it. "Maybe my Mother will let me share my bed with you some night, Renate. I will ask her." Renate has similar thoughts.

The next morning, we awake to the loud roar of engines. Sounds like airplanes. Quickly we dress. The Brahms are outside already and point to the railroad station. "We just saw airplanes. They were flying low above the railroad station, two planes," says Fraeulein Brahms. The hum of the airplanes returns, and we hear bursts of machine guns. We even see flashes of light. The next moment the planes resume altitude and disappear on the horizon. Anxiety overcomes us all. We don't know what to do. Should we go to the basement? We all look up, searching for more airplanes. But all remains quiet. We decide not to go far from the house today. We are also afraid to walk to the railroad station to gather the news.

By noontime, there is a loud knock on the front door. We recognize the same man who escorted us to the Brahms. He brings a couple and two daughters. The Brahms are requested to avail the two vacant rooms in their house to these German-Hungarians. They come from the train that was attacked this morning. The Browncoat tells us that the planes were American and that there was one casualty. "Murderers," he snaps.

The welcome this family receives from the Brahms certainly is much friendlier than our reception had been. This morning's scare just may have brought the Brahms a little more in touch with reality. Or maybe just the presence of a man influenced the Brahms' attitude toward the Wanukas.

Among themselves, this German-Hungarian family speaks Hungarian. The older girl Antje is 17 years old. She is beautiful and wears big, brown-rimmed glasses. She has long, blond, curly hair. Marisch is 13. Her freckles match her straight, light brown hair. I am envious of the beautiful clothes they wear. Mr. Wanuka is tall and has a mustache. He looks very dignified to me. He is well mannered. I don't know how to act around Mrs. Wanuka. She is very refined. In her presence, I feel uneasy, like I am being constantly assessed. The only time she speaks German is with Fraeulein Brahms. I heard her talk about the attack on the train. She said suddenly, the airplanes were there, and they heard the shooting. Then everything was over as fast as it had started. She said that one person was dead, and several others were injured. Hearsay had it that the planes were Americans. "Thank God that our family was spared. And thank God for the good shelter we have now and the good landlords," she says. No, I think, the addition of this Hungarian-German family will not improve Mother's relationship with Fraeulein Brahms.

I avoid Antje. Something about her ways is as arrogant and distant as her mother's. Arguing comes naturally to her. Marish is easy to take to. But her German vocabulary is so limited. Body language accomplishes more and works faster than verbal communication. It also makes us giggle a lot. Marish's father suggests that we seriously set aside some time every day to learn each other's home tongue. We receive this idea with enthusiasm. In addition to the fun, this interchange of words produces, our progress is rewarding. Herr Wanuka is pleased when I ask him in Hungarian, "What time is it? When do we go to the village?" I also try conversing about shopping and the weather in my newly acquired "Magyar" (Hungarian) knowledge. And Marish shows off her better German speech.

I believe that the German-Hungarians began fighting on the German side in 1941. There were many Germans living in Hungary on the western border. But why would a train full of refugees be attacked? We just never did find out. We know that the bombing raids over the metropolitan cities in the western part of Germany had killed thousands of people already. We know this for sure from local people who have relatives living in Leipzig and Frankfurt and Hamburg. They all are living in deadly fear in those cities.

Obviously, the Brahms benefit from and like the skilled help given to them by Mr. Wanuka. He knows how to fix anything in the house and the field equipment. Mrs. Wanuka does most of the cooking for her family on the kitchen stove. She always busies herself after our noon cleanup. They eat in their own quarters upstairs. I can't figure out where their food supply comes from. They sure must have loads of money. Maybe they are given a lot of food by the Brahms.

Never mind, I think. We are broke. We are not as free as we used to be. If only Mother would not be so down ever since we had to flee from home. I hope we will somehow soon be with Papa. Mother built a blockade around her and I don't know how to break through it. Only Frau Brunke is able to get emotionally close to Mother.

Wednesday morning is my birthday, April 25th, 1945. I am 16 years old. Frau Brunke invited us for a birthday party this afternoon. I am excited to see Renate. I am now legally qualified to hold a job. Renate has to wait two more months for her sixteenth birthday. Her brother Wolfgang has joined the local elementary school. Since there is no high school in Birnbach, Renate and I cannot attend classes.

Wow! Frau Brunke has some pear most poured for all of us. She toasts us with, "Hoch soll sie leben! (Cheers, for she is a jolly old fellow!)" From her landlord, she had negotiated a chunk of the sheet cake that came out of the big baking oven below her place just yesterday. The cake consists of yeast dough. Then it is topped with fruit or cream cheese. On top of that is a thick layer of streusels. It is delicious. Just like the kind Aunt Hedel always made.

Like always we are having the best time, talking and talking. There are always gripes about the "Natives", as we refer to them. Being a refugee means being on guard all the time. We have to continue to wait for the green light to signal us, to signal us for whatever lies ahead. Wolfgang tells us how the native kids call him "hunger skeleton". But he has new friends among the refugees that share his customs and background. Frau Brunke proudly shows off some china dinner plates, cups and kitchen utensils that she has been able to buy piece by piece.

Renate and I retreat to our foreign world of English on our leisurely stroll down the gravel road. We protest our refugee status. We pretend to be on a special assignment in a foreign country. Every time we pass some native people our English just pours forth, not always with kind remarks. We also notice that we have picked up quite a bit of the native dialect.

"I found out why so many women have that bulgy throat, Annemie. They say that it is caused by lack of iodine in the water. Nobody seems to be doing anything about it."

"What makes you think that we can't do as the Bavarians do," we exclaim with a pretty precise imitation of their dialect, as we enter the house. Our mothers find our performance quite original. Their talk focuses on the war situation. They know that the enemy activity on the Eastern Front is quite heavy. Many of the cities have fallen to the enemy or have surrendered. Details are not really known. But the latest concern is our immediate area. The Americans are advancing, according to the latest gossip. "Is this the calm before the big storm?" asks Frau Brunke. "Exactly in which direction are they moving? Where is the German defense?" replies Mother.

I would rather not know or hear about it. I like things better the way they are right now.

The glow of the sunset is fading already. A quick "good night" and an affectionate "thank you" sends us on our way home. The night and the stars are gleaming and Mother, at least for now, has put away the anxiety that I sensed during the conversation earlier.

The next morning, we awake to the loud and foul swearing of Herr Brahms outside. I look out of the window. I see an ox hitched to the plow. The slow going does not seem to satisfy him. I watch Herr Brahms lash out at the animal with his whip.

Maybe he avoids contact with people because he cannot treat them the way he treats his animal, I think. His face looks as though he is smiling all the time. What an artificial grimace! And all along I thought him sort of voiceless.

I crawl back into bed and pull the cover over my head. At home, I used to take noon naps right under the sky in the green grass. The nicest part about it was the carefreeness. I still can see the shepherd clouds float past against the blue horizon. I used to pick one cloud by the shape I liked and went floating with it. And sometimes I would leap from cloud to cloud. Maybe that is why blue is my favored color. What a melancholy world it has become now.

FINALLY

THE AMERICANS FREE US FROM WAR

The assignment for Emma today is to prepare the seed potatoes. I am in the barn to help her cut the potatoes. "As soon as Herr Brahms is done plowing, they can go in the ground," she says. "You can help, Annemie."

Today is the first time Emma talks about the war. She passes on rumors she has heard. Somebody had come back from Landshut by train. The American tanks were sighted outside of town. People are scared fighting could break out. There are still Nazi orders to defend the Vaterland to the end. "And those tanks are probably moving in our direction," she says. "How far is Landshut, Emma?" I ask. "Oh, about 50 kilometers." "And what are people doing about it?" I want to know. She doesn't know. I tell her, "We sure cannot run away. There is no place to go. I have heard it said that the Americans are not as atrocious as the Russians. And in the event of any fighting, we will just go to the basement. This building has such thick walls. It is just like a bunker." I am proud of my cool-headed strategy.

On the first Sunday of May the Brunkes stop by for a visit. They are not too comfortable with the short walk across the field. The word is out everywhere that the Americans are coming our way. Fraeulein Brahms even invites us all into her living room. She is not at ease with the spreading rumors. She is afraid of fighting and shooting. "I hope no German will show hostility toward the Americans," says Mother with distaste.

"I hope so too, Frau Guderian. I want this war to come to an end. And I hope no one gets hurt anymore," adds Frau Brunke.

"So, we just surrender," Renate offers.

Frau Brunke is irritable. "What are you saying, Renate?" Renate repeats her statement, this time in German.

Mr. Wanuka silences everyone. He says, "That is a good idea. We surrender. How can we lose? Would you avail one of your homespun white table clothes, Fraeulein Brahms? Annemie and Renate could then hang on to each end and carry it like a flag. They can become the angel ambassadors of surrender. They can peacefully meet the American tanks upon their arrival."

"Sure, those girls are not your daughters, Mr. Wanuka. My daughter will not have my permission to carry out that mission. Basta! (And that's that)." Mother speaks out in anger. Frau Brunke sides with Mother. Renate and I think the idea is great. We plead and reason with our mother and convince them of the worthiness of that mission. Eventually, everyone supports this plan.

"I hope our instinct and judgment will prove right when we meet our liberators. But for now, I don't want to waste more time. Let's go home, Renate and Wolfgang." Mr. Wanuka offers to accompany the Brunkes on their walk home.

Upon his return, he makes it known that the Brunkes are waiting for his word. He promises to keep an eye on everyday events. "As soon as there is any sign of Americans approaching Birnbach", he says, "I will bring the Brunkes here. Preparations for the decisive moment can then be made."

Mr. Wanuka plans with such confidence. Nobody questions his leadership. We all trust his decisions. He urges us not to go far from home. We all hope for the end of the war to happen soon.

***

Fraeulein Brahms prepares a sleeping place for Frau Brunke and Wolfgang in the living room. Herr Wanuka is bringing the Brunkes here this Monday evening. I get to share my bed with Renate. Fraeulein Brahms is even ironing her best white tablecloth. Renate and I recite, "We surrender, we surrender." Our mothers are sharing their concerns about the uncertainty ahead of us.

It is late by the time Mother comes to bed. Renate and I are too excited to sleep. Mother's thoughts return to home. She makes it clear that we are returning home as soon as possible if God lets us come out of this one alive.

The following morning, we all gather at sunrise in the kitchen. "How can we be sure everything is going to take place as we expect it to?" asks Fraeulein Brahms, turning toward Mr. Wanuka.

"We cannot be sure. But we have reason to think that this invasion or, we should say, liberation, is going to be a peaceful one. I have not heard of any violence on the enemy's side nor of any resistance by the Germans."

Mr. Wanuka is finishing his milk that Fraeulein Brahms serves to all of us this morning. "You all stay in the house. I want to see if there is any activity outside." We watch Mr. Wanuka walk towards the road that leads to Birnbach. The sky is cloudless, and the first sunrays warm the now green countryside.

Even Herr Brahms is nervous. His bushy eyebrows move up and down and he keeps wiping his nose with his shirtsleeve. Fraeulein Brahms is very quiet. She clearly is terrified. Marish sits on her mother's lap with her arms around her. Wolfgang is holding on to his mother's hand. All ten of us are waiting. At this moment our differences have disappeared and together we are afraid while awaiting the beginning of a new life.

The logical thing to assume is that the Americans would come down the main road leading to the railroad station. The other road out of Birnbach to Untertattenbach serves the small farms where Emma lives. For now, we just have to wait and hope for the best.

The wait for Mr. Wanuka's return seems like an eternity. But it is just over an hour when Mother nods in the direction of the road. In the hallway, our eyes meet Mr. Wanuka as he comes through the door. He is out of breath from his brisk walk.

He reports "Birnbach is empty of people this morning. I found a few in the Gasthof. There I got information that American tanks are rolling toward Birnbach. Nobody had any knowledge how much longer they would be in coming. People are apprehensive about the ending of it all.

"I still think our concept of surrendering peacefully is a goodwill gesture." Again, we find Mr. Wanuka "s coolheaded judgment reassuring. "I should think that before soon you two English speaking girls will have made history," he goes on. Renate jokes, "I promise, I will not set the street with the tablecloth," and she breaks the uneasiness that we all feel.

"So, this is Tuesday, the 8th of May 1945" Mother interjects. Our troops invaded Poland in September of 1939." On her fingers, she counts the number of years that have passed. "Five years and eight months ago." And with a deep sigh, she continues, "Who would have thought that it would last that long and bring so much pain, suffering, and destruction to so many people?"

"May we try the "surrender flag" outside?" asks Renate. We get permission. It stretches at least four and a half meters between us. We raise our arms as high as we can. Then we shout in unison, "We surrender!"

We have not been outside very long yet when I discover some movement toward the direction of Birnbach. I point that way. Renate turns pale. "They are coming. I can make out a tank moving. I am scared." "So am I, Renate!"

Mr. Wanuka is right behind us. And so is everybody else.

"Your meeting and greeting them will make them feel

welcome," he says.

Renate and I are now determined to carry out our mission. Slowly we continue walking toward the gravel road. Once on it, we stretch the cloth between us and raise our arms high. While the tank rolls our way, it is slowing down. My heart starts racing. Two men in brown uniforms are on top, looking down at us.

"We surrender!" we call out.

They smile at us and wave their arms. "Heil" they call. A second tank follows. The soldiers on the second tank also wave and call something that sounds like "heil" again. The tanks, some five of them, continue to move across the river and toward the railroad station.

"It is all over! The war is over!" Everybody behind us shouts at once. There is laughing and crying at the same time. Emotions bob up and down like a teeter-totter. "Renate, why did the soldiers say "heil"? Were they scornful? Did they mean Heil Hitler?" "That puzzles me too, Annemie. I don't know why they said that."

***

The Brunkes are with us on our walk to Birnbach today. We feel more comfortable being together. We expect to find the mood in Birnbach changed. We don't know what to expect. From the first house in the village comes a lot of laughter. It appears that the Americans are occupying it. Soldiers are in the yard. It is hard to understand what they are saying. We recognize one man from the tank. He is saying "heil" again when he sees us. Hesitantly Renate and I say, "Good day." "How are you?" he says. We nod our heads. He shakes his. "You are supposed to say: Thank you, I am fine. And, how are you? Repeat," he continues. "When I ask you again, you answer just like that."

The soldiers obviously are very pleased with the way we catch on. "Okay," we hear them say a lot. They seem to be everywhere. We notice their smiley faces and friendly ways. The atmosphere sure has changed from uncertainty to calm. People are seen throughout the village. They stand in small groups.

Voices are still kept low. It does feel more comfortable to stroll through Birnbach today than it did feel in the past.

We already think of the Americans as being kind and being friends. When they talk to us, they smile. We do not see them as our enemy. They are our liberators.

The sign in the bakery window reads "Sold out – try tomorrow." We go back home by way of Untertattenbach. Renate grabs my hand saying, "I will meet you halfway across the pasture around 7 o'clock or earlier, Annemie." "I will be there Renate," I promise.

***

"As soon as the transportation system returns to normal, we will be on our way home, Annemie," says Mother. "The money I have left should be sufficient to pay for the journey. I wish we could leave tomorrow. Maybe Papa is already back home. I would rather never have to go back to the Brahms. And I can't find anything in common with the Hungarians. Frau Brunke and I will stay on top of things and we will all travel home together soon."

At this time our future really excites us. We dream about being in our own home with Papa again. At suppertime, Fraeulein Brahms seems joyous. "Now that the war is over, you are going home, aren't you, Frau Guderian? It will be so good to have the house to ourselves again. When are you leaving?" and she doesn't hide the enthusiasm in her voice. Mother's icy response is, "Don't worry, Fraeulein Brahms. If possible, we would leave immediately. I myself can hardly wait to get away from here."

Renate says that it is all right with her Mother if she spends the night with us. She walks back with me and we sit on the bench in front of the Brahms' house. On the road, near the bridge, two soldiers are walking around. Both Renate and I would like to speak with them. We are afraid though to walk up to them. "Let's try to get their attention," I almost whisper to Renate. "I know what we could try. The only English song I know is 'Pack up your troubles in your old kit bag and smile, smile, smile.' Do you know that one, Renate?" "Yes, Annemie, I remember it." So, at our full lungs, we whistle that tune. Before we are finished, the soldiers have traced the sound and wave in our direction. We wave back and see them heading our way. We are too excited to move. "Heil," they say again. "How are you?" "Thank you, we are fine and, how are you?" I say. They ask whether we live here. We really have to listen carefully, and it is still hard to understand them. Their English does not sound like our teacher's did. In time we manage to slow their speech down. We do grasp quite a bit of what they are saying. We also miss some of it. They talk about America. We learn how they love their country. They are lonesome for home. We let them know that we are lonesome for home also. As best we can, and with heavy use of our hands, we try to explain about our homeland to them. We tell them that more than anything we want to go home.

James says with sadness, "The Russians are occupying your homeland now. You won't want to go back there." Then his face lights up and he almost shouts, "Come to America. There is no place on earth like it." Listening to them knots up my stomach again. I think we and the Brunkes have built a high, wooden fence around reality. We don't want to or can't accept that we may not be able to go home.

Their names are James and Bob. They learn from us how scarce food has become. It is too hard to explain how we have to depend on every single meal from the people who have to provide our temporary shelter. They will bring us some cake donuts tomorrow. We have no idea what they are like. They explain. Our mouths are watering.

"Why do you always say 'heil' to us?" I ask. "Do you think we are Nazis?" They both start to laugh. "Oh no," James says, "that is our customary greeting. It is a short way of saying 'good day'. It is spelled 'hi'. He writes it down on a piece of paper for us to see. "Now we understand," I say.

"May we come back tomorrow night?" asks Bob. "It is fun to talk to you."

***

The view from the Brahms' house has changed. Jeeps are moving in both directions on the road. Soldiers are exploring along the river bank. Mother carefully guards me and pretty much confines me to the immediate area. She allows me to meet Renate again half way. Our commutes help to keep the path down among the taller grass in the pasture.

As we sit on the bench we wonder whether Bob and James will come again and bring the promised food along. They are driving up with a jeep today. "Hi," they say. "How are you today?" They allow enough time for us to answer. "We brought you some cake donuts." The carton contains six donuts. Our watering mouths devour one immediately. "They taste so good," we thankfully tell them. I would like my mother to taste one and Renate would like to save one for her mother and brother.

"We will bring you another pack next time and some candy bars."

Bob and James talk so freely about their country. They point toward the river and say that they do a lot of fishing and hunting at home. We are impressed. It is only the very wealthy who can afford both the fishing and hunting fees here in Germany. Back when I was in grade school it was rare to see a man in his grey wool hunting suit with a "Loden" overcoat.

"You must be very rich," I blurt out. Bob laughs. "Oh no, I farm with my Dad in Nebraska." "You what?" He points to the land and the fields and pretends he is driving a car. "Oh, you are a peasant!" He nods smilingly. "Your English sounds so different from the English I was taught in school. But your English sounds almost easier."

James is an actuary. We cannot quite figure out what an actuary might be. We finally conclude that he is some kind of insurance agent. They both talk on and on about their families. They are both single, but they have girlfriends. James turns to Bob. "It is time for us to go. Good night girls. We will see you around."

In the room, I take a deep breath and tell Mother what the two soldiers have said to us. Germany evidently will be divided into four zones: Russian, American, British and French. It is obvious that Breslau will be in the Russian zone. "I know Mother; I want to go home as badly as you do. But the immediate possibility of returning home looks bleak at this time. We just have to wait it out for now."

Looking out of the window this rainy morning, Mother decides to make a change in our living arrangement. Frau Brunke had let it be known to her that in her landlord's main house a room was just vacated by two refugees. The Buergermeister (mayor) has approved the room for new occupants. So, Mother is seizing this opportunity for a move. It is not a difficult goodbye for Mother. I hear no more than "thank you and goodbye". I make more contact. I shake their hands and tell them that I liked living here.

On moving day Brunkes help us carry our few possessions across the pasture. Our "new home" consists of the same size room with two beds, a table with two chairs and a small wardrobe. The added luxury though is an iron potbelly cook stove.

"Now we have the stove but no food to cook on it, Mother." "Oh, we will try to get a pan and something to put into it, Annemie. We survived until now. We will struggle through the short while until we can go home."

On our past visits with the Brunkes, we had already been introduced to the landlords, Herr and Frau Hoeftl. They are a couple in their early forties. They have no children. Herr Hoeftl's mother lives with them. Frau Hoeftl explains that their mother is bedridden. Their house is arranged just like the Brahms' place, a wide, cobblestone entry hall. Rooms lead off on both sides. The first door to the right opens to a large pantry. Huge woven baskets are filled with eggs. Big ceramic dishes hold cream. Milk jugs, flour sacks, sugar, canned fruit, cheeses, and jams line the shelves. Smoked pork and sausages hang from the ceiling hooks. There is a barrel of sauerkraut and a keg with a tap. That, of course, holds the standard beverage, the pear cider. This looks just like a grocery store. My mouth keeps watering at the sight of all this wonderful food. Our room is next to this larder. Directly across is the kitchen. It is one big room. One almost bumps into the free-standing range. The surface offers room for many pans and pots. An enormous steam noodle pot with the wooden lid sits right in the middle. We are to get our warm water supply from the built-in tank. This is a good-sized farm. The sick grandma has her room at the end of the hall. Her door is always closed. The Hoeftls sleep upstairs.

It feels good to live so close to the Brunkes. We have become such good friends. We are just like one family. After a cup of Hagebutten (rosebud) tea at the Brunkes, Mother and I prepare for our first night in our "new home." As we crawl into our featherbed we find ourselves matted down on straw. Instead of a mattress we sleep on a burlap bag, filled with straw. "Let's pretend we are cows, Mother." "Just shift around till you are comfy, Annemie. It is not all that bad."

In the morning upon awakening I find myself scratching everywhere. "Are you itching like I am, Mother? I slept all night. I think I scratched myself in my sleep too. I must have been too tired to wake up. I have bumps on my arms and some on my legs. What could that be, Mother?" "I hope there are no fleas here, Annemie. They are so tiny. We could never find them." The subject changes to breakfast. We are allowed to help ourselves to firewood from the woodpile outside. This farm also shares the barn and living quarters under one roof. An additional large building is directly across from the house. It houses the crops and machinery. The Hoeftls have horses. They also employ help. Frau Hoeftl spends a lot of time in the kitchen to prepare meals for all the hired help.

"What's for breakfast, Mother?" I want to know as I drop the wood by the stove. Mother says, "I will ask Frau Hoeftl right now whether I may buy some bread and eggs from her. When we go to Birnbach later, we will pick up our rationing cards that we are entitled to now. From what I understand, refugees, living on their own are allotted certain food provisions free. Our money reserves are dwindling in a hurry. We just have to get back home soon."

Frau Hoeftl is not about to sell any food to us. She needs the supplies for her own family and farm help, she lets Mother know. But she offers to sell a quart of milk every other day to us. We also may help ourselves to potatoes that are stored in the barn. We can have a cup of coffee this morning and she gives us an end piece from the bread. Mother toasts the bread slices on top of the stove.

"We will never be part of them. We will always be foreigners to them," is Mother's remark. "Time to start fending for ourselves."

***

The distance to Birnbach is the same as it was from Brahms' place. A steep hill halfway to the village makes walking a little more difficult. Renate and I are ahead of our mothers. We have to reach the top of the hill before the village comes into view. Our Mother's immediate concern is for food. We hope to bump into Bob and James for some conversation. And sure enough. They notice us as we walk past "their" yard where they are working on a jeep. They introduce us to their fellow soldiers and we repeatedly respond to their "how are you" greetings. We, in turn, introduce our Mothers to them.

The shopping expedition turns out to be a big disappointment. The bakery is so short of flour that they drastically reduced their daily output of baked goods. The butcher shop does not even have that good smoky smell to it. It is empty. But some people come from the hardware store with ten-liter pails. We also buy a pail. It's a practical addition to our few possessions. At the general grocery store, we find some salt and pepper, some Kekse (cookies) and sugar.

On the way home, Renate and I remove our wedge sandals. They are not easy to walk in. The wooden rigid wedge doesn't bend at all. We let them dangle from our hands. We walk in the grass alongside the road. By the end of May the sun has warmed the earth enough to make her feel warm and fresh against the soles of our feet.

The Bavarian dialect keeps my conversation with Renate flowing. "You know, Renate, why can't we go begging for food just like the city people who come from Munich? If we talk the Bavarian dialect and pretend we are from Munich, maybe it will work." "Great idea, Annemie. Let's see what our Mothers think of it." "Give it a try," our Mothers uniformly declare. "We have to eat!"

We look forward to our new venture. We keep reciting and perfecting our Bavarian dialect. We all agree to the genuineness of the native tongue we produce.

Having knit shopping bags in our hands, both Renate and I set out on our solicitation tour. We walk along the road for more than an hour. We choose the opposite direction from Birnbach. We mustn't be recognized by anyone. The first farm wife we talk to believes our story.

"Greet God," we begin. "We were bombed out in Munich. Our families just live in one room. We don't have anything to eat. Do you have any mercy for your fellow Bavarians? We would so appreciate something, anything to eat. We have no flour for cooking and baking. There are no eggs to be had anywhere. A bit of bread would keep my little brother from crying with hunger. May God reward you for your good deed."

The woman listens to us and really seems touched by our story. "I will see what I can spare," she says. "How are you going to carry it?" We show her our bag. She disappears. When she returns she asks us to wrap the ten eggs individually into the paper she hands to us. She fills one paper bag with flour. Then she cuts half a loaf of bread and adds a homemade sausage. She also pours a glass of milk for us to drink. "Oh, thank you so much. Our Mothers will cry with happiness and pray for you. Greet God." With this Bavarian greeting, we leave. Our spirits are high as we are walking on the gravel road again. Good thing we are wearing our boots.

We are hiding our food alongside the road in tall grass. With our empty bags, we continue down the road. Almost unbelievable to us, we fare as well at the next farm. The second bag filled with more bread, flour, eggs, and some smoked pork. We can hardly wait to show everything to our Mothers. They cannot believe their eyes. "How did you accomplish this?" they ask. "Oh, it's easy. Just do as the Bavarians do; we burst out in our convincing Bavarian dialect."

When I awake the next morning, I scratch myself till I start bleeding. "I am not sleeping on this straw mattress another night, Mother. I have so many little bumps on my body. I am going to sit on top of the table with my legs pulled up tonight. Mother has far less bumps on her. She says, "There must be some kind of bugs in the straw." We search and look inside the burlap bag, but we cannot see anything.

Mother asks Frau Hoeftl whether we may exchange the straw in the bag for sleeping. She says that it can wait a week. It should be good for two weeks to sleep on before it mats down. But she explains where to dump the old straw and stuff it fresh in the barn. So, we watch for her to leave. When she does, we quickly go to the barn. We thoroughly inspect and shake the empty burlap bags before we refill them. We do that now on a weekly basis. It appears that there is no longer a problem.

"Tomorrow may I make some noodles at your house, Frau Brunke? Your table is bigger, and I know that you have a rolling pin. I have watched Fraeulein Brahms often enough to know how to do it." We save our milk for that feast. There is sugar to sprinkle over the thick soup. Hmm, milk and homemade noodles! Potato pancakes are now our daily main course since Renate and I have been able to provide the flour and eggs. Since Frau Hoeftl refuses to sell us eggs, we help ourselves occasionally to them. Mother sewed an apron for me with a pocket in front. That is where an egg or two go when I get our little milk jug from the pantry.

Mostly Renate and I are gone from four to six hours on our "begging expeditions." We must be careful not to be recognized. Some days we do better than others. The added food supplies help make our daily existence more endurable.

The native people are clearly not accepting us refugees into their community. I think to myself, they have not suffered any hardship throughout the war. They have not lost anything. They did not have to leave home like we had to. They had enough to eat. Why can't they be nice to us? They just don't understand. Hopefully, we will be on our way home soon.

***

In Birnbach, the dairy has resumed operations. Word gets out fast that buttermilk can be purchased. So, Renate and I walk to Birnbach every Tuesday and Friday. Our big pails are half full. The road is hot and dusty during these July days.

Many times, we meet men clad raggedly. They ask whether we know of a woman or children by such and such name. These former fighting soldiers don't know where to find their families. Their homes used to be anywhere east of here, just like ours did. Now they don't know where they belong and how to learn about their families. How forlorn these former German soldiers look. Aimlessly they try to find their way, shuffling along in an unknown direction.

I think back to the children on the train, whose mothers were left behind. Will they ever be united? And where might Papa be?

"Do you wonder where your Dad might be right now, Renate? Don't you wonder when and if you will see him again?" Renate stares into the distance. "I am lonely for him. I wonder if he will ever teach again at the same school. I am lonely for school, too."

The whistling comes from the American soldiers. They are busy in the yard. James walks toward us and soon other soldiers follow and crowd around us. They are so eager to speak English with us. They offer us candy. Young children from the village are watching the soldiers. Standing right behind us is a tall black man. He has the whitest teeth and the most sparkly eyes I have ever seen. I cannot take my eyes off him. Never before have I seen a black person. Back in school, I learned about Negroes. The kids surround him with outstretched hands. James comments that the kids just love him. He is so generous and has a way with them. James puts a bunch of candy bars and donuts into our pails. He says he will take a drive with Bob to our "new" place some evening. Then we can talk some more. He kiddingly adds that we will have to learn to speak "American".

On the way back, we carry the buttermilk pails as though they hold precious jewels. For dinner today: mashed potatoes and buttermilk. What a treat!

Mother says we were notified to come to a meeting next week. America is sending care packages. They will be distributed to refugees. Our share consists of milk powder, dried egg powder and two cans of cherries. We also are to try on shoes. Mostly they are Oxfords, white and brown. I can't even fit my foot halfway into the shoe, nor can Mother or the Brunkes. All these shoes are so narrow. Only a few people are lucky and find a pair that fits. Our feet are so wide. Maybe our many barefoot walks have spread them out. Twice a month we are treated to these gifts of the American people. The staples are always packaged in green and white twisted cotton sacks. Mother sees a potential use for those threads. "That thread will knit into sweaters and pullovers," she says. So, at the next distribution, we ask for all the extra-large sacks that were used for shipping. These supplies will keep us busy forever, I think. "I like to knit, Annemie, you too?" "I do, Renate."

So, we set out to the slow task of unraveling the thread. What a test of our patience. The knitting that follows is much more pleasant, even though we can only use thin needles for the thin thread. A sweater grows from our moving hands. Renate and I take turns sitting up with our knitting at each other's homes. The bed is the most comfortable place to sit hours on end into the night. Mother rations the candy bars from James and Bob. So, there is always a little treat every night.

We all sit together when we knit and talk and dream about being home again. Wolfgang has turned into such a domestic boy. Whenever he notices a crumb on the floor, he goes after it with a broom. We joke about his good housewife qualities, but it rather annoys him.

It is late this evening and I go into the kitchen for some warm water. I turn on the lights. I stop breathing. In horror, I look at the biggest bugs I have ever seen. They are all over. They are on top of the stove, they are crawling on the walls, and they are everywhere. I have to keep myself from screaming. I just touch the light switch with one finger and I am back in our room.

"What happened Annemie? Why are you so white in the face?"

"Don't ever make me go in the kitchen at night again, Mother. I turned on the lights and these big, really big bugs were crawling everywhere. I have never seen anything worse. What are these big animals?" Mother explains, "Sounds like they are cockroaches. They only come out at night."

"Yuk, all my hair is still standing on end. How come the Hoeftls don't get rid of these miserable bugs." I am so frustrated. I want to run. Run nonstop, far away. Mother consoles me. She says that we will put a rag tightly under our door every night to make sure no bug can crawl in.

Renate and I spend long hours knitting. When we finally wear our home knit sweaters, compliments come our way. Some of the native people would like a pullover, others a vest or a jacket. They want to know how long it will take. "It depends on the pay," we halfway joke. They negotiate seriously. So we knit and we knit. We sit up late into the night. For every finished piece, we receive a handsome food supply. Even the Native's money is beyond the reach of any material goods. There is just nothing available.

Many a night we hear the grandma's horrible sounding moans. "I bet she is being eaten alive by the bugs, Mother. I heard the doctor say to Mrs. Hoeftl that the infection is acute. I wonder what he is doing for her on his weekly visits. I see him walk out with meat and sausages every time he leaves."

**

One day in Birnbach we overhear people speaking of the

abundant champignons. These mushrooms are only to be found in the early morning, before sunrise. They grow right in the pasture. So, we are up at dawn the next morning. In no time our big pail is full. By the time we are home the mushrooms are so packed down, there is just a quarter pail full. The native people don't eat them.

"If only we had butter to fry them in," Mother wishes.

"I will offer to pile wood for the Hoeftls," I say. They gladly accept my help. I ask for cream in exchange. We pour it into a bottle and shake it for a long time. It works. Butter has formed inside. It is a challenge to remove the butter through the narrow bottleneck. But finally, bits of butter are on the plate.

Frau Brunke fries diced onions in the butter and then adds the mushrooms. We pile them on to a thick slice of bread. What a feast for the five of us! The main meal is always at noon when Wolfgang comes home from school.

Another day all of us take a hike into the wooded hills in search of blueberries. "The first berries should be ripe. It is the end of July already." And as we approach the blueberry patches, Frau Brunke continues, "Look at all the berries, how plentiful they are. And they are just about ready for picking." They taste so delicious. We can't swallow them fast enough. We finally are so full. With our mouths blue and our hearts happy we start to sing "The Happy Wanderer" on our way home.

A few days afterward we pack sandwiches and head for the woods with our big pails. Mother, Renate and I plan to quit picking only when the pail is full. At day's end, our backs are sore, but the harvest is good. Frau Brunke has cream of wheat waiting for us. How delicious with the blueberry sauce we just made. We don't even wait for it to cool down. Some of the berries we trade for cream and eggs.

So time passes. Talk often turns to home and our Dads. We have reported our whereabouts to the Red Cross in Munich. The Red Cross is beginning to actively match people who are looking for lost family members. Of course, now we wait anxiously for mail every day.

***

This morning Mother and I start out for the railroad station. Through the pasture and past the Brahms' house we walk. Actually, Mother wants to find out about train schedules; where do they go to and what are the fares. There is no travel to our home province of Silesia. We are told that Silesia is under Russian administration. The official thinks that any area east of the Oder River might be ruled by the Russians now.

"Will we ever make it home again? How much longer do we have to hold on to this uncertain life?" Mother drops on the bench almost with exhaustion.

"Where are you from?" a lady asks with curiosity. She listens with interest and sympathy to Mother. "So, you are refugees. Just hang in there. Someday things will get better for you, too. Things are pretty rough now. I was born and raised in Bavaria. But after I met my husband we immigrated to the United States. He was a head waiter at a nice restaurant in New York. My sister also lives in New York. Then we came for a visit. My mother in law was very ill and passed away. She was a widow. So, my husband inherited the house. This all happened before the war began. So, we got stuck here. We do plan to return to the States someday. I would like it if you came to visit me. I can fix some waffles. My name is Frau Lukas and I live in that white house over there." She points to that beautiful white house against the hillside, the same place that caught my attention immediately when we arrived here by train. "How about tomorrow," she asks. Thankfully, Mother accepts. "What a nice lady. And she even is Bavarian. I can't believe she invited us, Mother."

Through the pasture we stroll, during the midday sun, to visit Frau Lukas on the next day. To me, the house looks like a small castle from a fairytale. It is so immaculate. The colors are light with a lot of painted borders. The living room has the customary border benches. Most of the wooden furniture is ornately carved and painted white. The colorful flower borders look great against the backrests.

Frau Lukas has a waffle iron. She makes such good waffles. She serves them with strawberries and whipped cream. I have never eaten waffles before. She tells us how this is a breakfast dish in America. As the afternoon moves along we talk about many things. Frau Lukas shows such interest in our life events. It bothers her that my school education has been interrupted. She explains that the nearest high school is in Passau. Passau is on the Danube River, some 50 kilometers northeast of here. But there is a qualified Professor in nearby Pfarrkirchen. She goes on to say that I could earn a high school diploma if I am willing to study hard. And she keeps stressing the importance of education.

On our walk home, the thought about my education occupies us. "I surely would like you to continue your schooling, and better yet, get your diploma," says Mother. 'We will ask Frau Brunke's opinion."

"Someone is coming across the pasture, Mother. I have seen that man before when I walked with Renate."

"Guten Tag," he says. "Madam, it would be a pleasure for me to give your daughter a pair of shoes. Every time I see her, she is barefoot. What size does she wear?"

I see Mother swallow. "Did I understand you correctly? You just want to give my daughter a pair of shoes?" "Yes Ma'am, no strings attached. I temporarily live in Pocking at a camp with my Jewish countrymen. We are waiting to be relocated. When may I meet you to deliver the shoes?"

"In exactly one week my daughter and I will be at the railroad station around two o'clock."

Jubilantly, I become the owner of a well-fitting brand-new leather shoes, precisely one week later. "You are God's proof of love and the goodness of mankind. You must be sent from heaven. May your happiness be limitless. Thank you." "My pleasure, Madam," and he is gone.

***

Frau Brunke listens to Mother's account of the education program we had just been acquainted with. Both Mothers agree that it is important to see to the girl's education. Pfarrkirchen is just 7 kilometers away. "Let's inquire about a train pass and the educational program. The girls maybe could share the books. If we can possibly afford it, let's consider it," they agree.

Both our Mothers return from the meeting with the Professor in Pfarrkirchen with optimism. They already signed us up to begin in September. A three month, hard-working course will award us a high school diploma. "Yahoo!" echoes from both our lips.

"You only have to ride to town twice a week," we hear our Mothers say. "But understand that you have to set aside a lot of time for study. Now you really need to put your minds to work. Give it all you have! We know you both can do it. No matter what, you will take this project very seriously." The Professor is a big source of knowledge. He has a lot of faith in the future. We plan to work hard.

Luckily Mother has been able to buy a piece of fabric. With her good seamstress skills, she has been hand sewing a few things for both Renate and me. So at least we don't have to be ashamed of our appearance. There are more people learning from the Professor. Even two young men are among them. Their education had also been interrupted because of the military draft.

***

It is the middle of October when the mailman brings that long awaited letter. Papa is alive and resides in Hannover. Mother is so overwhelmed by this good news, she breaks out into sobs. And I am just overcome with joy. Our worst nightmare is over. We will see and be with Papa again soon. We carry on and on with joy till we start trembling. It is so hard to contain our happiness.

There is so much to write about. We keep the letter short as though we expect to get it there sooner that way. On the way to school, the letter to Papa is dropped at the Post Office in Pfarrkirchen. We hope to shorten the mailing time that way. We want to hear more from Papa and want to know that he is all right.

Two long weeks and a day go by before Papa's reply reaches us. He writes, "Dearest Hella and Annemie, my prayers have been answered. Getting a sign of life from you is still a miracle. I thank God for saving my family. I am so excited. I pray for patience until I can hold you both in my arms. I hope that we will be reunited soon. I live in one room here. I have a job. We will have each other. How much more do we need? I inquired at the railroad station and was told that it is better that you make reservations from your end. So, get busy. Come on home as quickly as possible. In the meantime, you both are in my heart as you have been all these years. – Love, Fraenze and Papa."

"Now we can make real travel plans, Annemie." Forgotten for now are my studies and Mother's cares. We are off to the railroad station. We more run than walk. "If you want to travel to Hannover soon, maybe even this month, I suggest you go by freight train," the ticket agent says. "They are running on a more regular basis. I know for sure that three cars are designated for Hannover. You never have to leave the car until you arrive at your destination. I can take your names. I will notify you as soon as the dates are available to me. I expect it to still be in November." Mother instantly agrees to that arrangement. "We are in control of our fate once more." She is elated.

"Your studies will be completed before this month is up, Annemie. What perfect timing. How will Frau Brunke take it?" Mother worries. Frau Brunke is happy for us. But her frustration and sadness are there. So far, she has not had a sign of life from her husband.

***

This Thursday, November 22nd, is our last school day with the Professor. The day is gloomy, and the first snowflakes begin to fall. Renate and I carefully hang on to our money. One hundred German Marks hopefully will be exchanged for our diploma. We hope that we both passed our examinations.

"You have studied diligently the last twelve weeks and you are both deserving of the High School Diploma I hand to you now. My best wishes and success for your future, Annemie and Renate." With that, we are dismissed.

Our happy feelings are overshadowed with thoughts of parting. It is almost more than we can bear. On the train back to Birnbach, we let our tears flow. After that, we feel some relief.

In the meantime, Mother finalized our travel arrangement. "The ride to Hannover will not be as painful as the one that brought us here," I am assured by her. The car might even be empty. It has a wooden bench and even a potbelly stove. Firewood is stacked right in the car. We can keep the fire going to keep us from freezing. There will also be a small window in the car," so Mother was told.

On Sunday we have our last good waffle dish with Frau Lukas. In her realistic way, she bids us goodbye with lots of good wishes and her blessings. She hands her address as well as her sister's in America to me and tells me to write to her and also to her sister, in English. "You are a good woman," Mother expresses from her heart.

Monday evening Frau Brunke has supper for us. The mood is beyond sadness. I feel like I am on an elevator. It constantly goes up and down, nonstop. I can't stop my feelings. They bob up and down. That's how it must feel when you go crazy, I think. Frau Brunke has our new address.

A "goodbye" and "thank you" is not that emotional with the Hoeftls.

In the early afternoon this November Tuesday the Brunkes walk us across the pasture to the railroad station. It is a most quiet walk. We know what is deep in our hearts. We don't really have to talk. Two bags easily accommodate our few possessions. Just a very long embrace with all before we disappear into the car. We feel the slow motion already.

Dusk is slowly breaking. We want to look out at the passing world. Our eyelids are too heavy. So we sit on the bench, leaning against each other. We just let go. Our hearts are so full. So many sad thoughts, so many new expectations.

We are being awakened with, "Hannover Hauptbahnhof (main station)."

"We don't want to wait on the platform. Let's go inside the Station." Mother walks toward the steps already. "We should look around for Papa," she says.

"I don't know what Hannover is like. I know that in size it must be Breslau's equivalent," she adds. "It is only 7 o'clock in the morning. That is most likely why there is not much activity. Will Papa find us? Annemie, can you believe that we parted almost six years ago? Why don't you step outside and look around? I will stay here. Don't be gone too long though."

It is a long Plaza outside. Streetcars are moving in all directions. There are lots of gaps between the buildings. I don't think that the City was originally built like that. It enters my mind that these gaps might be the result of dropped bombs.

I have been out here long enough. Papa is nowhere in sight. I better go back in, so that Mother does not become worried.
As I enter the Station again, I see them both. Both Papa and Mother are standing there. I join them.

It is time to stop worrying. I feel secure. I think to myself: nothing can ever, ever come between us again. I want to really believe that the past years were just a dream.

From the streetcar, we witness the destruction the war has brought upon this City. The two- and three-story rubble piles are still boldly stretching into the sky. The air raids destroyed countless living quarters, leaving many residents homeless.

The Potsdamer Conference (consisting of the Three Heads of Government of the United States, Britain, and Russia) gathered to decide how to administer the defeated Nazi Germany, which had agreed to unconditional surrender nine weeks earlier, on May 8th, 1945. A Central Allied Control Council for Administration of Germany divided the Country into four occupation zones. The American, British and French zones made up the Western two-thirds of Germany. The

Eastern Third being controlled by the Communist Russians.

Papa says, "Life is still far from normal. The whole country is changed. The housing shortage is the biggest problem. All people who were lucky enough to escape the now Russian-controlled zone are competing for the limited available housing in remaining Germany. You have already experienced the Americans. The British and Americans are the best. At least we are far enough away from the Russians."

We get off the streetcar. It is just a short block to walk to the apartment building. Up the steps, we climb to the fourth floor. Papa's key opens the apartment door. The room he lives in is tiny. The three of us can barely move around. The sight from the window is ugly, nothing but a mountain of ruins.

"My landlady has a friend living across the street. She is willing to lend her living room couch for you to sleep on every night, Annemie. She says the offer stands until we can find better living conditions."

Papa is already into his daily routine. He walks to the office. He was transferred to Hannover. He is a tax official now.

"Will we ever go home?" Mother asks pensively.

"The true answer is: no. We don't want to live in Russian occupied Germany. We have to accept that." Papa continues, "We have our memories. We are preparing a new future together. We will build a new life!"